Catholicism

Catholicism: Religion of Tomorrow?

BY HENRI FESQUET

TRANSLATED BY IRENE URIBE

HOLT, RINEHART AND WINSTON

NEW YORK   CHICAGO   SAN FRANCISCO

Library of Congress Catalog Card Number: 64-21931

Designer: Ernst Reichl
82795-0114
Printed in the United States of America

To those men and women who, although they do not believe in Christ, have helped me to understand him better.

Contents

Contents

Introduction

Most mistakes come from using the conjunction "or" instead of the conjunction "and."

Marshal Lyautey

I owe everything to the Church, and nothing can affect me save through her.

Georges Bernanos

THESE PAGES have been written by a Catholic journalist for those half-believers on the fringes of the
Church, for that numberless species of marginal
Christians who say that they have "lost their faith"—
rather as one loses an old umbrella, not too regret-
fully. Our purpose is to present some aspects of
Catholicism as it exists in fact today, embodied in
the Church—that Church which people daily en-
counter in the persons of its faithful, clerical and lay,
and which for twenty centuries has aroused men's
hate or love or indifference.

3

We will speak of the Church candidly and without false modesty, veiling neither its grandeur nor its shame. We will neither flatter nor disparage. The shortcomings of Christians, starting with those of the clergy, are obvious enough to dispel any temptation to minimize or exaggerate them. We need only look about us to find stupidity, pettiness, formalism, pretentiousness; but also, if our vision is not blurred, intelligence, heroism, and the astounding vitality of a Church to which so many still turn their eyes and stretch their hands in times of loneliness and anguish. With a faith that moves mountains, a small nucleus of ardent Catholics works unremittingly to show all those who thirst for justice and love that Christ is, as he said, "the way, the truth and the life," and that the Church is still, with all its vicissitudes, his vehicle from age to age.

These pages are addressed to free minds. We cannot bother about sectarians, whether religious or irreligious—there are as many of them in one camp as in the other. To sophistries and apologetic contortions, we prefer the unvarnished truth. Truth and courage build up what cold calculation and cowardice have torn down. The plain fact is that Catholicism has become unintelligible to the modern world. And that, in our view, is rather the fault of Catholicism than of the world.

The Church of men is made up of cockles and of wheat; its countenance is sometimes distorted, sometimes smiling. Many have been disillusioned by the mask they have encountered, and have turned away, hurt perhaps forever. Then there are all those Christians of good will who have suffered at the hands of the Church, and who are too readily taxed with pride, when what is needed is to bind up their wounds and to practice a little self-criticism. The breed of the Pharisee is immortal.

Since God is invisible, he can always be pictured according to one's fancy; the Church, however, presents an obstacle. That is the necessary price of the Incarnation. The Church, upon occasion, will stand upon its transcendence, monopolize the truth, disdain the modern world. Theologically, of course, the oft-repeated assertion of the Church's "holiness" and "spotlessness" is valid enough; yet in practice many priests and laymen have been scoundrels, and thanks to them, the Church has failed in vast sectors of the world.

It may be quite useful for a Catholic—a mere layman, one among many—to take it upon himself to speak of the debit side of the Church's ledger; humbly, of course, for every Christian feels himself coresponsible with his brethren, and remembering, too, to speak of the other side. After which we shall attempt to underscore certain features of Catholicism which seem to us to correspond best to the aspirations of our contemporaries.

The extent of religious ignorance today is astonishing; it borders on the incredible. Take all those "confirmed" and practicing Catholics who know virtually nothing of the rudiments of their faith or of the inner life of the Church. Or take all those Catholics whose secular culture is on a very high level, who have attended universities and graduate schools, yet whose religious culture is virtually nonexistent. The tremendous disparity is symptomatic of our modern civilization, whose soul has shrunk as its body has swelled. It is hardly surprising that faith should have deserted the masses, when even those intellectuals who were baptized Christians most often remain at the infantile level of a badly taught catechism, and know sacred history only in the form of nursery tales. Can we wonder if they are embarrassed when the topic of their religion is brought up, and if they are ashamed of their creed, convinced as they are that the Church's doctrine is but a hotchpotch of old wives' tales?

To be sure, there has been some observable improvement. A small number of active Catholics are beginning to take their adult faith seriously. But as against a handful of baptized Christians who have taken the time and the trouble to come to an informed opinion, there are many more who base their views on prejudice or on contempt. Theology, of which they know only the trimmings, they regard with total indifference. Intelligence, it would seem, has abdicated before the things of faith. And those who wish to think out their religion in terms of the realities of their time are regarded with rank suspicion.

Countless people today keep up with the latest currents of thought and science, yet never so much as open a religious book or periodical; they feel that it could not possibly interest them. They do not even suspect that judiciously chosen reading might enrich them and clear away certain apparent obstacles on which they have always foundered.

The result of this negligence is all too predictable. Faith withers; religious practice, if it survives, becomes a social formality or a purely sentimental gesture; preoccupations of a political nature encroach upon the field of action, slowly but surely warping religious judgment. Or, if a man has a more or less mystical temperament, he will construct a private religion which leaves the Church out of account. Inevitably, he will waste time "reinventing" what already exists, instead of using his creative energy to push forward, and he will isolate himself unnecessarily, and not without damage to himself, from the Catholic community.

Recent Popes have dealt with this problem *ad nauseam*, but few people seem to care, or even to know.

"Doctrinal instruction is what is most needed in France at the present time," Pius XII told Mgr. Theas. And on another occasion, the same Pope told his listeners: "Know how to answer for your faith. Your religious culture should be proportionate to your secular knowledge."

Pope John XXIII, in his first encyclical, had this to say on the subject:

If so much effort and industry are spent in adding to the store of human knowledge and to pushing back the horizons of natural science, so that this our age rejoices, and justly so, in the remarkable progress that has been made in scientific and philosophical knowledge, why should we not show the same ingenuity and assiduity, nay even greater, in acquiring in a safe and certain manner that knowledge that is concerned not with the passing things of this world but with the heavenly goal that is to come?[1]

Why such lack of interest? It is often said, not without some justification, that the fault lies with the public school, or with secularism, or with something else. We must be honest enough to recognize the poverty of such explanations; Christians ought first to accuse themselves. Just as Protestantism would never have arisen had the Church reformed itself in time, so unbelief and prejudice against the Church would never have become so widespread had

[1] *Ad Petri Cathedram* (Glen Rock, N. J.: The Paulist Press, 1959), p. 9.

8

Introduction

Christians been able to show that theirs was a culture open to the modern world, and had they been more anxious to combat social injustice. Fr. Tavard is absolutely right when he says:

"Too many ignorant journalists distort the texts; too many priests understand them poorly and explain them even worse; too many catechisms, pamphlets, posters, simplify them beyond recognition; too many instructions and pastoral letters present doctrine so one-sidedly that prodigious good will and ingenuity are needed to understand them. . . ."

These pages will contain nothing that is startlingly new. We shall simply repeat what we have had the opportunity of hearing or reading. Our job, as a journalist, is to popularize, to serve as a relay, at the risk of being incomplete or superficial. The Church's "public relations" are badly handled; we might even say that they are nonexistent. This is unfortunate, for, while the Church does not need advertisement or propaganda, it does need testimony. Like God, the Church needs men, men of our time who speak to men of our time in the language of our time.

"The Church has enemies among its children, and children among its enemies," wrote St. Augustine. We are grateful to both. To those who are Christians without realizing it; to believers whose faith and zeal light up their own lives and the lives of those around them; to the nominal Christians, too, whose indifference has spurred us on.

We shall refrain from judging, that is, from condemning. We shall merely describe and inform. We
shall try to avoid the temptation of "do-goodism."
God's ways are not man's ways. True religion is a
matter of love. And love, the alpha and omega of
Christianity, can flower only in an atmosphere of
freedom; at most it can be fostered after it has come
upon us like a thief in the night. God, if he exists,
asks only that we be transparent to his grace and
that we do not try to elude him.

The Debit Side

Because of the ignorance and the
weakness of its members, the whole
Church can say each day, "Forgive us
our trespasses."

St. Augustine

1
Intellectual
Mediocrity

> My people perish for want of knowl-
> edge! Since you have rejected knowl-
> edge, I will reject you from my
> priesthood.
>
> Osee 4:6

PROPHETS ARE indeed a trying breed of men. And if
their fellow men are so prone to kill them, it is obviously because they do not want to listen to them.
Time was when clerics set an example of erudition.
They were the bearers of civilization; they, in
troubled times, preserved learning in the havens of
the monasteries. Thanks to them, too, culture slowly
spread among the people. The public school has
done no more than carry on this Christian tradition,
giving it a broader scope.

Those days are gone indeed. Certainly there are a

number of Catholic scientists, philosophers, and theologians today who are an honor to mankind, but they are not much honored by their fellow Catholics. From Catholics they have received more rebuffs than encouragement. Where are the "patrons" of old? Does the Church of the twentieth century no longer need scientists, philosophers, theologians?

Even in France, where the position in this respect is probably better than in some other countries, original thinkers are suspect. By its antiquated procedures, the Church has succeeded in bringing its best sons into disrepute, those who really believe that they have something new to say, the only ones, possibly, who would be capable of giving renewed youth and vigor to a Church which they love above all else. One could cite many examples, both recent and painful. The attempts to disguise the facts or to justify them have failed.

Pope Leo XIII's remarks to Mgr. Hulst are very apposite in this connection. He said:

There are anxious and churlish minds who urge the Roman congregations to pass judgment on doubtful questions. I am against this. I stop them. For scientists must not be prevented from working. They must be allowed time to hesitate and even to make mistakes. The truth can only benefit. The Church will always be in time to set them on the right path again.

The Debit Side

Writing in 1914 of the intellectual mediocrity of a part of the clergy, Mgr. Mignot had this to say:

A wave of disaffection from us is everywhere in evidence among thinkers and scientists. . . . Within the Church itself, discouragement has gripped the intellectual and social workers. . . . Their task has become exceedingly hard, because they are regarded with suspicion by persons who have been deceived by false reports into casting occasional doubt on the purity of their motives. The clergy have no understanding whatsoever of the intellectual and moral difficulties which surround them, or of the movement of ideas, to the great detriment of the Church. The clergy will remain static in the midst of a world on the march, a world of which they are supposed to be the light. Neither their minds nor their hearts will seem open to those who are assailed by doubts, and who need them so badly.

Who would dare assert that this description no longer fits, despite certain signs of reform? It is not that the Church no longer has men of real ability; the question is whether, except in certain religious orders, such men occupy positions where they can be most effective, where they can use their talents to the full. We sometimes hear that pastoral letters or bishops' instructions are not sufficiently known or read. The complaint is justified, and the fact is re-grettable. But the reason, possibly, is that these documents are not always of the keenest interest, and that they rather dully reiterate commonplaces which fail to hold the reader's attention.

It is never possible, of course, to generalize without injustice. Nevertheless, it is a fact that when a bishop happens to publish a remarkable series of pastoral letters, they are immediately translated into several languages and discussed in every circle. And it is also a fact that this unwonted success stirs up virulent jealousies.

No one would deny that the curriculum in many seminaries is inadequate, or that the teaching of important subjects is neglected—for example, Church history, the development of dogma, modern philosophy, the contribution of psychoanalysis, pedagogy, sociology. The theology taught in the seminaries is "textbook theology." We have known establishments where seminarians were forbidden to supplement their textbook (and what a textbook!) by using a library during study hours. The result is that where moral fiber is weak, intellectual curiosity gradually atrophies, and a frightening grade-school mentality develops. The cleric no longer even suspects his own ignorance, and later he will go forth into the world uttering false prophecy, despising those areas of which he knows nothing, convinced that he "possesses" the truth. Most of us have suf-

The Debit Side

fered from such inadequacy on the part of priests—
an inadequacy allied with utter complacency—and
suffered, too, from the gaps in their culture, the
ponderousness of their judgments, and especially
their passion for lecturing without even trying first
to listen to and understand the person they are talking to.

The teaching of religion reflects this state of affairs. The mediocrity of the seminaries leads to the
mediocrity of catechetical instruction. Too many
priests still disregard biblical pedagogy and cling to
the recitation of set abstract formulas, which leave
the child cold and gradually turn him away from
religion.

A few years ago, the following courageous and
distressing statement on catechetical instruction appeared in the bulletin of the diocese of Strasbourg
(it was published in *Le Monde* on July 22, 1959):

We must honestly admit to the partial failure
of our religious teaching, despite great good will,
honest effort, and sincere attempts to improve our
methods. . . . The lack of discipline, the use of
unsuitable methods, the premature introduction
of the text of the catechism, the misuse of certain
teaching aids which are perfectly valid if used dis-
cerningly (pictures, film strips, stories, etc.), the
cult of words, and in some cases a misplaced
emphasis on learning by rote—all this prevents

the instruction from influencing the children's lives. More pains are taken to get through a syllabus than to nurture the students' life of grace.

Stubbornly, but in isolation, certain priests have set about renovating catechetical instruction and transcending the anachronistic quarrel between the Catholic school and the public school which masks the real problems. These efforts are still in their infancy, and we have long to wait before they bear fruit. Our grandchildren will doubtless be amazed that their forefathers should have argued so long about the public school instead of concentrating on procuring an equitable status for chaplains in the lycées, increasing their numbers, and improving their training. While the Church may conceivably stop teaching the secular disciplines, it cannot stop teaching the Gospel and Christian doctrine without betraying its most sacred mission. Those who attacked these problems in the past, or applied themselves to changing the prevailing attitudes or structures, were subjected to endless harassment. Yet they were doing no more than taking seriously the complaint of Pope Pius XI that "Christian doctrine is negligently taught or the obligation of teaching it is shirked."

"The greatest danger to the Church," Canon Cardijn said, "is not Communism. It is that the workers know nothing of the Church or of Christian doctrine." What is being done to remedy this ignorance? We need only recall the fate of the worker-priests, who were encouraged at first, and then suppressed. The heroic obedience which one of them—the finest among his peers—showed his superiors caused him literally to die of grief after a terrible nervous disease.

The greatest danger for the Church is that *everything* is not being set in motion to remedy the mediocrity of seminary training and thereby the ignorance of so many Catholics who no longer realize that ideas rule the world and that holiness is no substitute for competence.

Cardinal Suenens, Archbishop of Malines, had good reason to write, "There are sins of inertia and intellectual laziness which will weigh far more heavily on the day of judgment than sins of frailty."

Intellectual laziness is not peculiar to the rank and file of the priesthood; it flourishes in the high echelons too. It is common knowledge today that one of the chief reasons why the members of the French episcopate were so anxious to suppress the Holy Office's letter condemning outright the whole worker-priest venture was its "theological weakness." When one of the most important "ministries" of the Church reaches that point, and when, at the same time, the rights of bishops in their dioceses are flouted for all the world to see, certain reforms would seem imperative. Christ's teaching turns against the very people who have been officially commissioned to preserve it and to pass it on. "For it must be that scandals come, but woe to the man through whom scandal does come" (Matthew 18:7).

2
Contempt
for Truth

> God does not need our lies.
>
> Leo XIII

Is THE CHURCH the seat of truth? Every Catholic worthy of the name believes it is and cannot hesitate to profess it. But this certainty is precisely what makes the occupational disease of certain priests so much more irritating—we refer to their lack of intellectual honesty.

When he teaches catechism, the priest tells the class that lying is forbidden. Nevertheless, acting on the principle of "do what I say, not what I do," many a priest has no sooner left the classroom than he proceeds from half-truth to half-truth in the attempt to cover up—not very successfully, be it said—the failings of the ecclesiastical society. The Catholic religion passes sometimes for a school of hypocrisy. The reproach is not entirely unfounded. For the failing is specifically "Catholic." Protestants, who are often more scrupulous, are also quicker in self-criticism.

We will deal only with the so-called "edifying" lies. On the pretext of not giving scandal or of wishing to justify the action of a particular priest or prelate or tribunal, how many untruths are calmly advanced, how many sophisms painfully elaborated, what virtuous contortions practiced! Sometimes it takes years, if not centuries, for churchmen to admit to wrongs, blunders, monumental errors. Sometimes they never admit to them at all. To vindicate the "cause" of the Church, to consolidate its position in the world, to ward off some too searing rebuff, how many lies are heaped up by the very people who teach the Decalogue! Most of us have read, or tried to read, books of apologetics bent on proving that the Church has never been wrong; that if it seems to have been mistaken, it is only because the incident has not been considered in perspective or from a sufficiently lofty viewpoint.

Fr. Gabel, the former editor in chief of *La Croix*, once wrote: "The human quality of Christians is not unaffected by the ability to discern the truth, to accept it and defend it, even if it does not correspond to the interests of their sociological group, which interests are all too easily identified with the cause of the Church and the kingdom of God."

More recently, Cardinal Feltin, addressing the

members of Parliament of the Fourth Republic, used
language applicable equally to the practices of the
Church and to those of political circles: "Truth has
inalienable rights. They can be violated or disre-
garded for a time, of course; they always prevail in
the end. . . . It is no less necessary to speak the truth
and do it than to accept it. . . . I realize that certain
deceptions or frauds have no other purpose than to
reassure or soothe public opinion; but even so, is this
always wise? Will not the awakening bring about an
even more cruel disappointment? Is it really loving
others to foster their errors or illusions?"

What shameful pressures are put on this or that
religious publication to induce it to color the facts,
to lie by omission! How many "denials" are issued,
similar in every respect to those government "denials" which have never fooled anyone!

We might cite this little dialogue which took place
recently in Rome between a Vatican priest and a
French layman:

"What is the percentage of nonpracticing Catholics among Romans?"

"We have no idea," answered the priest. "But even
if we knew, we would not give the figures out, because that would weaken our position with the Com-
munists."

All too often the priest is not disposed to respect
the truth. It is a matter of training. He does not
really understand the desire for unbiased informa-

tion. He has no "feel" for democracy. He thinks it permissible to "lie to the people" provided it is in a "good cause."

Not every truth, of course, is to be uttered indiscriminately, at all times, and to everyone. It is normal to put off the publication of some news or to disclose certain facts cautiously if public opinion is not prepared to understand their full implications. But these provisos, dictated by common sense, are badly abused in practice. More often than not, this is an almost unconscious process, resulting from fear or pride; they do not want it said that the Catholic Church—a society made up of men like any other human society—is capable of error, even outside the sphere of faith and morals![1]

We said that hypocrisy was a peculiarly Catholic failing. The priest, indeed, is accustomed to teaching a doctrine which he is sure is true. With all his soul he believes that he belongs to the only Church which is fully authentic. Little by little a curious shift of emphasis takes place, a sort of transfer. The truth which he teaches goes to his head and he ends up believing that he is himself infallible, that he,

[1]"Catholics are not Catholicism. . . . The faults, the dullness, the deficiencies and the apathy of Catholics do not implicate Catholicism. Catholicism is not supposed to provide an alibi for the failure of Catholics. The best apologetics is not to justify Catholics when they are wrong, but on the contrary to point out where they are wrong. . . ." (Jacques Maritain, quoted by Mgr. Ch. Journet in *Théologie de l'Eglise*, Descleé de Brouwer.)

The Debit Side

too, is an "absolute." Thus he confiscates truth and cuts it down to his own human size—a hideous perversion, which makes of the Christian religion not what it ought to be but the exact antithesis—that is, a school of caste, of exclusiveness, and of contempt.

3

Contempt for Human Dignity

The methods of investigation used by the Holy Office show too little regard for human dignity, a cause which the Church takes every opportunity to champion.

André Latreille

"THE INALIENABLE rights of the human person," "respect for the human person"—these are standard expressions in the Catholic vocabulary. And who would find fault with that? Particularly in our day, when we are beginning to realize, schooled by hard reality, that Christ is the best friend man has, and his teaching the only one, perhaps, which takes account of all the contradictions of man's nature.

Yet what violence is done to these great principles in the daily life of the Church! We do not have to go

26

The Debit Side

back to the Middle Ages, to the Inquisition and its burnings at the stake, to Joan of Arc or John Huss. It is hard to see things in their proper historical context, and to avoid the presumption of judging a past period by the standards of the present. Let us consider only our own times. Can we say that intolerance and fanaticism are dead? What are we to think, for instance, of the cynicism with which the Church in certain countries makes itself a party to the persecution of Protestants, on the pretext that such action is in the interests of the State? Where are the official protests against policies which take us right back to the sixteenth-century wars of religion?

Then there are the cases—more serious still, perhaps, since they involve the Church's own children —where the Church appears to be almost indifferent to the psychological traumas that may result from an ecclesiastical decision which shatters a reputation or a position. What has become of certain priests whose only crime was to be consumed by apostolic zeal or by a longing to initiate urgent reforms?[1]

The answer which is sometimes given—but it is

[1] François Mauriac wrote: "I shall not hesitate to denounce the scandal from which I have suffered all my life: the incredible indifference, within the Church, to individual disasters resulting from certain decisions; all those souls thrown overboard! This is as true of the clerical world as of secular society. Does the Holy Office worry about the repercussions its decrees may have on the lives of zealous young Catholics, clerical or lay?" (*L'Express,* October 20, 1952.)

too facile—is that the Church does not condemn persons but erroneous ideas, suspect books or undertakings. But how is the distinction to be made in practice, how is the one to be condemned without besmirching the other? No one questions the usefulness of a kind of police whose duty it is to stand guard—lovingly, if possible—over the purity of doctrine, and to track down dangerous trends. No one denies the occasional need to prune, to cut away. But why should this not be done with the sensitiveness of a mother rebuking her child? Why not do everything possible to correct before striking? And if it becomes necessary to strike, then why not do it discreetly? Why not warn the person concerned? Why not take real trouble to "enfold" the culprit, once it has become impossible not to penalize him? Why all this silence, these sword thrusts in the shadows, these schemings which sometimes savor of revenge? Why all this brutality which makes the heart—and the mind—bleed? Where, in all this, is the charity of Christ? Do not some of the methods of censure discredit the censors themselves? We cannot but recall these words of Jesus: "Blind guides, who strain out the gnat but swallow the camel!" (Matthew 23:24) Or again: "Woe to you . . . because you load men with oppressive burdens and you yourselves with one of your fingers do not touch the burdens" (Luke 11:46).

Fr. de Lubac, who, like so many others, has had to

The Debit Side

suffer "misunderstanding for the Church," writes
with restrained emotion:

There are some milieus in the Church that fur-
nish a particularly favorable breeding ground for
calumny, and once it has taken root there, it feeds
not only on the worst but also on the best. Even a
sincere and mutual desire for the good—even for
the same good—does not prevent tragic clashes; it
can even provoke them, as can be seen from the
lives of the saints. And the strangest and deepest
of hurts, without parallel in purely human experience, become possible when, within this unique
form of association, some men possess the awe-
inspiring power of exercising pressure upon others
at that most deeply personal point of linkage
where soul and intellect divide; when there even
exists a power so strong and deep-reaching that
merely to submit to it, even with patience, is simply not enough—that we have to consent personally and willingly to what would be a violation at
the hands of any other power. For this is precisely
the situation into which Catholic obedience, in its
most common form, takes us.[2]

Fr. de Lubac's authority, and the genuineness of
his spirituality, make it unnecessary to labor the
point.

[2] Henri de Lubac, S.J., *The Splendor of the Church* (Glen
Rock, N. J.: The Paulist Press, Deus Books, 1963), pp. 54, 55.

We must have the courage to say all this, and say it loudly, because all too many priests and laymen think it and say it under their breath. A Christian worthy of the name cannot but suffer from the defects of his Church, cannot but struggle, at whatever cost to himself, to banish them. Fortunately, throughout the ages the Church has always raised up submissive and respectful sons who were prepared to sacrifice their personal convenience for the sake of purifying its countenance. True love cannot be cowardly. It would be well, sometimes, in hours of crisis, to have more striking proof of this.

4

The Church
and Mammon

We ask you, my lords the successors
of the Apostles, not to give offense to
the poor man who is seeking Christ.
Léon Bloy

THE FACT that the overwhelming majority of the
French clergy are poor, and that most of them live
simply and sometimes heroically, does not do away
with this problem, which remains one of the blem-
ishes on the face of the Church. Reputations die
hard. Catholicism, as is only just, is harvesting today
what it sowed in the past. By amassing wealth, sometimes on a very considerable scale, by occupying luxurious palaces, by habitually cultivating the rich and
powerful rather than the poor, the Church has
heaped coals on its own head.

It would be untrue to say that the Church is not

concerned with the poor. It has done and is doing much for them, lovingly and without fanfare. But it would be still more untrue to claim that it was doing all that it could in this area and that this was its principal preoccupation, as the Gospel requires. Sporadically, yes, but globally, sociologically, no.[1] The Church is trying, as best it can, to make up for lost time. But lost time can never be completely regained. And so many reforms are still pending, tucked away in files. How hesitant Rome was about countenancing the worker-priest experiment! Perhaps the project had been inadequately prepared and organized. Nevertheless, following Rome's ban on the movement, we find ourselves in the incredible position of witnessing the complete repudiation of the most imaginative effort of the apostolate in our century. The French cardinals were clearly dismayed. In suffering silence they are waiting, apparently, for better days. But when will those days come? There was no lack of men prepared to work out more satisfactory arrangements, no lack of men in favor of launching the venture again on sounder foundations. Why were they not taken seriously? The years go by, and the "scandal" denounced by Pius XI persists: "The Church has lost the working class." That is the class which holds the key to the future, which tomorrow, perhaps, will man the con-

---

[1] "In the great majority of social conflicts," wrote Fr. Couturier, "Catholics were very generally on one side. And it was not the side of the poor."

trols. A working-class civilization is taking shape, and the Church has no part in it; in this emerging world the Church is neither known nor loved. It is not enough to say that the scandal persists; it is growing more grave.

As long as bishops live in luxurious houses in residential neighborhoods; as long as they spend most of their time at official ceremonies, surrounded by hot-house plants and red carpets, in places where the poor man cannot feel at ease; as long as they ride in expensive automobiles; as long as they do not step down into the streets and mingle with the crowd as Christ did, the vast army of the poor will not believe in the Gospel. France was lucky enough to have an exception at Lyons—a bishop who was also a crafts-man. But Rome forbade him to work.

The poor man is not open to argument or verbal justifications. He believes only what he sees. We can always explain—and mostly it is true—that the man behind all this pageantry leads a simple and austere life. It does not register. John XXIII realized this admirably. He invited workmen to his table, went about Rome on foot, visited prisons and hospitals; nor was he prepared to accept a merely symbolic washing of the feet on Maundy Thursday. Pope John's popularity was due in part to his democratic manner. We may hope that this was only a beginning, and that the day will come when the higher clergy of Rome will live in a setting more patterned on the Gospel.

Let it not be objected that the ecclesiastic must keep his rank, that he must set himself apart by exterior signs which will impress the masses, that he must be able to command respect. This is no longer true. The saints secured their prestige otherwise than by dressing up like actors in an operetta and surrounding themselves with liveried flunkeys—they did it by giving away all their possessions; by going away naked, as St. Francis did one April morning; by living in shacks, braving snow and wind, fasting, praying in the dust. Can we have forgotten the poor and simple life of Christ, of St. Paul, and of the Apostles, who mingled with the crowd of humble folk and sinners?

Some laymen are setting an example. Giorgio La Pira, the mayor of Florence, has never become a prisoner of the luxury which "ought" to surround his office. He lives in a cell and returns home in the evening barefoot, without a coat and without money, having given everything to the poor. Who will give the modern world all the La Piras it needs? Who will give the Church of France priests who will earn their own living? Who, among the clergy, will go beyond the formal vow of poverty, which passes completely unnoticed, and teach his brethren in the priesthood to lead a truly evangelical life?[2]

[2] The spiritual descendants of Charles de Foucauld—the Little Brothers and Little Sisters of Jesus—give a remarkable example in this regard.

The Debit Side

"Money," said a courageous prelate to whom all too little attention is paid, "money is the great sin of the Church." He was only too well placed to see the ravages made in his diocese because of certain priests' love of money and power. We are all aware, alas, that priests sometimes become expert in the art of extorting legacies, and that they take advantage of their influence as "spiritual directors" to acquire considerable sums. However, I knew a priest who refused money from a rich manufacturer for the reconstruction of a parish hall because he realized that his parishioners would not feel at home in it—an exception which proves the rule.

In any case, the Church is on the whole less poor than it is said to be. It collects considerable sums. However, these resources should be equitably distributed. Priests and bishops who preach so many sermons and write so many pastoral letters about fair wages sometimes take advantage of the loyalty of their domestic staff, their employees, or the teachers in the Catholic schools. The clergy are sometimes the worst employers. Moreover, they are so naïve in their choice of associates and so ill-prepared themselves for the intelligent management of funds that unbelievable wastage takes place—if not sheer misappropriation of funds by unscrupulous managers.

"But woe to you rich!" says the Gospel. This applies to societies and nations as well as to individuals, as the Chinese priest, Fr. Huang, points out.

Does the Church as a society really have the spirit of poverty? Who can truthfully answer "yes"?[3]

It is no accident that the rich countries are also the most selfish. It is no accident that the poor countries—and how can we help but think of the Mediterranean peoples?—should be the most generous and the most hospitable.

Priests who have to collect money know well that those who have least give proportionately the most. Those who are most comfortably off are the most reluctant to part with their superfluity. The blame falls in part on a Christian teaching which neglects the imperatives of social justice, and wrongly falls back on a pagan conception of private property. And there still exist Christian moralists who believe that peace is better served by sinking billions into the manufacture of nuclear weapons than by a disinterested policy of economic assistance to the underdeveloped nations.

Perhaps it is necessary to have been a worker-

[3] Pope John XXIII, in his encyclical on the occasion of the one-hundredth anniversary of the death of the Curé d'Ars, thought it opportune to recall these words of Pius XI: "We see every day how priests of humble life, who, by reason of the teaching of the Gospel, in no way work for their own interests, always gain marvelous benefits for the Christian people. . . . While we see men selling everything for money, and setting a price on everything, may these walk disinterestedly through the allurements of the vices, and, in a holy manner rejecting the unworthy desire of gain, seek the profit, not of money but of souls. May they desire and seek, not their own glory, but God's." *Sacerdotii Nostri Primordia* (Washington, D. C.: National Catholic Welfare Conference, August 1, 1959), pp. 8–9.

priest incognito to know how an ill-clad man is received when he knocks at the door of a suburban rectory looking for the least room in the servants' quarters so that he will not have to sleep in the public shelter any more. St. Francis of Assisi tells in the *Fioretti* how he found "perfect joy" when he was turned out by the monastery doorkeeper in the midwinter. And yet it is by these gestures of welcome, or their absence, that we shall be judged. Christ tells us: "Amen, I say to you, as long as you did not do it for one of these least ones, you did not do it for me" (Matthew 25:45). Without charity, all gifts—intelligence, culture, faith itself—are vain. Without charity, we are but "tinkling cymbals." Only charity will never pass away, and will save us.[4]

What the Church needs is another troubadour of poverty, a new St. Francis who will make the virtue of poverty and total detachment shine forth before the eyes of the world. That is really the great lesson which men expect from the Church, even if they do not fully realize it. For social justice itself is vain if those who benefit from it are not, or do not become, "poor in spirit." This is the paradox of Christianity. Feeding the hungry, giving drink to the thirsty, clothing the naked, is not really constructive, either for him who offers or for him who receives, unless the gift is made and accepted in a spirit of poverty. No one can serve two masters; no one can serve both God and Mammon.

4 Cf. 1 Corinthians 13.

The Credit Side

Man can very well fail the Holy
Spirit; the Holy Spirit never fails the
Church.

Fr. Henri de Lubac, S.J.

WHAT WE HAVE SAID in the preceding pages may be dismissed by some as a caricature. It is indeed a caricature, in a twofold sense of the word. For the Catholicism which we meet every day, the events and the men who shut themselves up in the daily round of mediocrity, these are a caricature. A caricature which we all foster within us to some degree. It would be both stupid and hypocritical to believe ourselves better than others. The sins of "others" are our own sins. The sins of the religious society to which we belong—and even if we do not belong to it

—are our sins, for every man is answerable for his brothers in time and space. We may not all be murderers, but we are all guilty, and no one can make excuses for himself by criticizing others, nor take comfort in such criticism. The consequences of original sin (the Christian explanation of the inclination to evil which has inhabited us since the dawn of mankind) weigh heavily on every human institution, even one ordained by God and watched over by the Holy Spirit.

It is a caricature, too, because this portrait of Catholicism, harshly drawn but not untrue, is only a mask. It is the deceptive mask which hides the true face of a religion watered by grace, the screen which stands between the anxious eyes of men and a Church which will endlessly disappoint and dazzle—an irritating and yet irreplaceable sign of contradiction. But it would be a complete misunderstanding to dissociate the visible Church from the invisible, to set the one in opposition to the other. To reduce the Church to an invisible society—as some more or less Manichaean idealists would have it—is really to reduce it to thin air. The Church, like Christ, is a living being whose soul and body are conjoined. The Church's hands are not always clean, but soiled hands are better than no hands at all. This principle is inherent in a positive, historical religion, plunged in humanity. It is the inexorable logic of the Incarnation.

It would be equally vain and wrong to set the hi-

erarchical Church over against the inspired Church,
the prophets against the spiritual leaders, the "spirit"
against "authority." This is a dangerous temptation
which opens the door to every error. To split the
Church in two is to mutilate its very being. The
only really successful "reformers" have worked from
within, realizing that, whatever the Church's "betrayals," no one has the right to rend its seamless
robe.

Has the Church betrayed its mission? Has it become the "great harlot" of the Apocalypse? What the
enemies of the Church forget, blinded as they are by
hate—which is often but a form of disappointed love
—is that the harlots in the Gospel story received
shattering favors and exceptional promises. Not, of
course, because of their defilements, but for the sake
of that adorable and mysterious element concealed in
every being who suffers, who is scorned, yet who is
also a party to his own degradation.[1]

The Church is indeed made up of all the defects
which we have pointed out, and of many more besides. But it is also—and pre-eminently—made up of
treasures of faith, hope, and charity, as every honest
and informed person must concede. In the twenty
centuries in which the Church has pitched its tent on
our barren soil, it has remained, for all its defects,

---

[1] The Church "is the Bride whose frailty is continually mani-
fested in the spiritual prostitution from which [Christ] continually
liberates her, purifying her by His union," writes Fr. de Lubac
in *The Splendor of the Church*, p. 65.

the great educator, the great civilizing force of humanity, and the imperturbable herald of the God-Man. Twenty centuries ago, the evangelical ferment first appeared in a Mediterranean cave in the shape of a child like any other, with no strength save his own weakness. Since that day, this ferment has been slowly spreading to the four corners of the earth. And in all that time, nothing—or virtually nothing—of what the Western world has achieved has been achieved, whether consciously or not, without the Church or independently of its influence.

Thanks to Christianity, the position of women has been enhanced; monogamy has become the rule; human love has been transfigured (one might almost say "invented" by Christianity); slavery has been outlawed; liberty and equality have become ineradicable ideals; hunger and thirst for justice have gripped men's hearts; even Communism is so tenacious a heresy only because it is a carrier of Christian values. Christianity was the first to teach men to distinguish between the spiritual and the secular powers.[2] It shattered for good the religious myth of the political potentate, who has ever since been regarded as a monster.

[2] It is true that the popes were temporal rulers for many centuries, and that they sometimes imposed their rule unjustly on kings; the theory of indirect sovereignty served as a pretext for a great deal of intervention in secular affairs. But in theory at least, sovereignty was divided between two powers, and the temporal gradually achieved autonomy, in contrast to what took place in countries ignorant of Christianity. Christ's statement, "My kingdom is not of this world," gradually bore its fruit.

The Credit Side

The doctrine, "Render, therefore, to Caesar the things that are Caesar's, and to God the things that are God's," despite countless misapplications, gradually gained ground. By separating the sacred from the profane, by distinguishing clearly between the relative and the absolute, by routing the false gods of clay or of mortal flesh, Christianity restored to the things of the world their true proportions. By placing them where they belong, that is, in the second place, subordinate to the one God, the omnipotent Creator, it finally delivered them from tyranny, ennobled them and, paradoxically, situated them in their right order and their own sphere of autonomy. The notion of the secular, however strange this may appear, is in the first place a Christian idea. We shall return to this.

The Church has been and remains the teacher of sanctity. From the first centuries it has produced the most perfect specimens of humanity. Bergson the philosopher was so struck by them that he spent a part of his life studying their lives, even though he was an unbeliever. The mystics and the saints, far more than the heroes and great leaders of peoples, have shaped the world and caused it to transcend itself. What would the West have been without saints like Benedict, Bruno, Francis of Assisi, John of the Cross, Teresa of Avila, Vincent de Paul, Ignatius of Loyola, Thérèse of Lisieux, Charles de Foucauld, and their disciples?

And should we not pay the tribute they deserve to

that great infantry of priests who heroically endure their solitude and give an example of sacrificial living and boundless charity? Bernanos would not have invented his *Country Priest* had such a priest not already existed.

Judeo-Christianity has delivered the world from the oppressive weight of fatality, from the chains of despair and futility. It has taught man hope. Since Christ, man knows that the wheel of history moves forward as it turns, that it cuts into virgin soil, and that progress is not an empty word. Only the Church —or its sister churches—has taught man that the world is something to be fashioned every day. It has taught him that only he can transform the world by transforming his own heart. It has given him confidence in the possibility of the spiritual and material betterment of human society. It has taught him the meaning of universal brotherhood. Jesus, the new Adam, first born of the new era, appears as the leader of a redeemed race of men, forever pardoned and washed of their defilements if they will only say "yes" to the voice that sounds within them. The most unbelieving, the most ignorant, the most vile of men, reaps the fruits—perhaps unwillingly as well as unwittingly—of this working capital of light which for twenty centuries has been reaching out to illuminate the whole planet. Only the Christian churches possess a peaceful army of missionaries. Only they have enough faith and love to announce the Good News to every living creature, to teach every creature that for him a God-Man once shed his blood, and that a bridge now spans heaven and earth.

Any unbiased mind will concede that the good done by the Church far outweighs the ill. After two thousand years of tribulations, disorders, sin, betrayals, and stupidities, the Church still stands. And it is stronger than ever since it gave up its temporal power. Never has the prestige of the papacy been as high as it is today.

A saying compounded of irony and realism has been current for generations in Christian families, and it is as apposite as ever today: "The best proof of the divine origin of the Church is that the priests have not succeeded in wrecking it!"

Of course, we must not delude ourselves. A constantly growing body of men knows nothing of the true face of the Church. People speak of the Church without any understanding whatsoever of its nature. Now it is an anachronistic survival in a modern world of technical efficiency, now a financial power whose sole ambition is to flatter the powerful or to extort pennies from the gullible. The Church is repudiated by myriads of people who delight in dwelling on the distressing features to which we have drawn attention. Worse still, myriads of working people are totally indifferent to religious problems in general. Even hatred is preferable to such tragic indifference. Please God, the Church's Roman general staff will realize it before too long and will permit the bishops to "carry the burden of their own responsibilities," as one French cardinal put it recently.

In middle-class circles, or more generally in circles other than those of the working class proper, some recognition exists of the efforts which have been made within the Church during these past thirty-odd years in the direction of theological, liturgical, pastoral, and artistic renewal. It is realized, too, that the intellectual cream of the nation is taking Catholicism seriously again, and that in the graduate schools, for instance, militant Christians are more numerous. The Church, through its Young Agricultural Workers (J.A.C.), is taking a leading part in the movement for rural renewal. The French Confederation of Christian Workers (C.F.T.C.) is also playing a more important part in the life of the nation. Is all this to be regarded as the final convulsions of a dying religion, or as the first burgeonings of a new springtime of the Church? The question is worth considering.

But first we shall draw attention to certain traits of Catholicism which are generally misunderstood. We shall do this particularly for the benefit of those who, out of ignorance or in all good faith, take the essential for the accidental, and *vice versa*. But neither shall we lose sight of those who, in the silence of their hearts, suffer on account of the Church.

What Is
Catholicism?

1

The Duty
to Think

It is not heart that is lacking, but
head.

E. Renan

We must love intelligence.

Fr. Valensin (on his deathbed)

"Woe to me because I dared think," wrote Monsieur
Pouget one evening in a moment of melancholy—
the Monsieur Pouget whom Jean Guitton has res-
cued from oblivion.[1] In contrast to the noble and
temporary discouragement betrayed in this heartfelt
cry, we may point to another, and equally genuine,
attitude. General Gissac, a practicing Catholic, said
one day, "When I enter a church, I leave my intelli-

---

[1] Jean Guitton, *Abbé Pouget Discourses* (Baltimore, Md.: Helicon Press, 1959).

gence at the door. I listen docilely to all that the priests tell me or order me to do, and I obey without seeking to understand."

Without realizing it, the General was contradicting the traditional teaching of the Church. For the Church has never asked the faithful—as the army sometimes does—not to seek to understand. On the contrary, it explicitly invites them to use their intelligence. The Church has no use for robots. Neither has Christ. Intelligence, referred to sometimes as the "daughter of God," is our noblest attribute. It has always been honored by the doctors of the Church and by the great theologians. The Church has officially repudiated philosophers who belittled the intelligence, which they said was incapable of arriving at truth by its own unaided powers. The Vatican Council condemned the fideist doctrines which taught that faith alone, a supernatural gift of God, enabled the intelligence to attain to particular rational certainties. The intelligence, wrote St. Augustine, has a capacity for God (*capax Die*).

The Church, in contrast to so many modern minds haunted by Kantian idealism, has thus become the defender of the rights of the intelligence. Against all opposition, it has upheld the intrinsic value of reason. We are therefore entitled to speak of Christian, or, even more accurately, of Catholic "rationalism," for the Roman Church has been almost alone in consistently, and forcefully, repelling the modernist temptation to substitute feeling for the values of the intelligence.

The Church makes it a duty for Catholics to use their reason. As a result, Christian philosophy and theology have been able to evolve in a dozen different directions,[2] philosophy being essentially the construction—by reason alone—of an outlook on the world at large; and theology being reflection—by reason, enlightened by faith—on revealed truth.

It is fashionable today in some circles to despise theology or to make fun of theologians. It is a fact, of course, that plenty of theologians, unmarked by brilliance, have juggled with abstractions, argued about the sex of the angels or, more recently, speculated on the possibility of sons of Adam living on the moon. The laughter of some unbelievers is not always unwarranted. The rights of humor and healthy criticism are inalienable too; certain mental exercises are ludicrous at a time when so many crucial problems have hardly even been touched upon. But the misuse of a good thing should never be cited as a reason for condemning it. Of reason, as of wine and of the tongue, we can make the best use, or the worst. God save us from sentimentalism, water-drinkers, and impenetrable silences!

Moreover, we have to be logical all the way. On what grounds, if not on grounds of reason, can

[2] *In dubiis libertas* (in doubtful matters, freedom), according to the celebrated maxim recalled by Pope John XXIII.

reason be condemned? The anti-intellectualists, if they have lost their faith, are turning in circles. And if they have not lost their faith, they are heretics in spite of themselves. It is better to observe the rules of our human condition and recognize that we cannot escape philosophy—or theology, if we are believers—without giving up the thing that constitutes the dignity of man. Only a better philosophy and a better theology can save us from a bad philosophy and a bad theology. Otherwise the door is open to all the excesses of instinct and feeling. "Refuse to try to know what you want, but want it just the same with all your might!" That is the absurd theory of the "activists," who scoff at those whose vocation it is to reflect and to understand. Despair is the only logical consequence of skepticism—despair with its sterility and its decay. Woe to those whose frivolity, vanity, and selfishness have so scandalized exacting but fragile minds that they have seen no other solution but suicide of the intelligence or of the heart!

By defending the rights of intelligence and reason, by giving full recognition to the position of philosophy and theology, Catholic doctrine is defending the basis of all civilization and all culture. To despise reason is to despise man. Catholicism carries on the tradition of the great philosophies of the past in raising the standard of the intelligence against all the disintegrating doctrines which would degrade man.

The Church has confidence in man, in all men of

all classes and of all races. That is why, basically, it has always rejected the notion of an aristocratic religion reserved for initiates. By seeking to teach the catechism to all the children of men, the Church laid the cornerstone of a democratic world. It destroyed intellectual servitude at its root.

Pius XI, among other popes, declared that "ignorance of Christian doctrine is the worst of contemporary ills." When the hierarchy so vigorously enjoins the faithful to know their religion, it is only carrying out one of the essential requirements of Christianity, one of the evangelical counsels; namely, not to hide one's light "under a bushel," and to carry truth and light to every man who comes into the world.

The catechetical renewal which is now taking place, the lengthening of the course of religious studies, the increased number and the success of theology courses for adults—these are unmistakable signs of the Church's determination to raise its children to a more appropriate level.

As for theology itself, the fact that a renewal is taking place is not sufficiently known. Theology is, or always should be, "in the works." Today, at any rate, the "works" are not idle. The emphasis—an encouraging sign of the times—is on what Canon Thils, of Louvain, calls the "theology of earthly realities," that is, the theology of history, of work (a major task which has barely begun), of the laity, of human love and marriage, of science and technology, of the universe, and of matter.[3]

The defense of the rights of the intelligence, as Catholic theology conceives it, leads to another conclusion which unfortunately is not yet generally accepted. Not only must human reason exercise its right to examine scriptural texts and the historical development of dogma, but it must also attempt a philosophical critique of the history of Catholicism and the development of its conceptual apparatus. This difficult task, initiated with great fanfare by Henry Duméry, whose works have been condemned, would have to be undertaken by a group of experts which has yet to be formed.

Exegetical criticism proper has already provoked a number of objections; nevertheless, and especially since Pius XII's encyclical, *Divino afflante Spiritu,* this difficult work has made noteworthy progress. There is today a school of biblical criticism whose works are universally esteemed. Rome has finally accepted them, with minor alterations. It is necessary to go further along this road, without excluding any possible development. Unfortunately there are still timorous spirits among Catholics who fear that criticism may undermine certain "traditional" positions.

[3] Fr. Teilhard de Chardin, as far as we know, was one of the very few thinkers who sought to grasp the implications of the mystery of transubstantiation (the changing of bread and wine into the Body and Blood of Christ) for the preparation of the Parousia; that is, for the progressive divinization of the products of human labor.

What Is Catholicism?

Does this indicate a lack of faith? Assuredly. Cardinal Newman expressed it perfectly when he wrote:

> In spite of the testimony of history the other way, they think that the Church has no other method of putting down error than the arm of force, or the prohibition of inquiry. . . . I say, then, he who believes Revelation with that absolute faith which is the prerogative of a Catholic is not the nervous creature who startles at every sound, and is fluttered by every strange or novel appearance which meets his eyes. He has no sort of apprehension, he laughs at the idea, that anything can be discovered by any other scientific method which can contradict any one of the dogmas of his religion. He knows . . . that if there be any one science which, from its sovereign and unassailable position can calmly bear such unintentional collisions on the part of the children of earth, it is theology. He is sure—and nothing shall make him doubt—that, if anything seems to be proved by astronomer, or geologist, or chronologist, or antiquarian, or ethnologist, in contradiction to the dogmas of faith, that point will eventually turn out, first, *not* to be proved, or, secondly, not *contradictory*, or thirdly, not contradictory to anything *really revealed*, but to something which has been confused with Revelation.[4]

[4] John Henry Newman, *The Idea of a University*, II, VIII (Garden City, N. Y.: Doubleday & Company, Image Books, 1959), pp. 421, 422.

Christianity has whetted man's appetite for truth. Christ, after all, defined himself as "the Truth." So far from faith blunting intellectual curiosity and discouraging the spirit of research, it should be a stimulant to the alert mind and an added and weighty reason for examining the soundness of accepted positions. Those whose vocation it is to "think out" the faith should be principally concerned to subject every facet of religion to the most searching criticism. In this area, more than in any other, timidity is a vice contrary to the essence of the evangelical spirit. The worst form of cowardice is to cling to an accepted position for fear of possibly upsetting this or that certainty. Intelligence is insatiable or it is worthless. Faith—a theological virtue—is intrepid or it is worthless. The logic of Christianity has no room for taboos. Enlightened by faith, human intelligence can dare all things.

In our day, when so many things are being re-examined—and our century can take pride in the fact —it would be catastrophic for the faith were we to refuse to examine religious "truths" with the techniques of modern science or philosophy. There is no better champion of one's interests than oneself; a religious society worth its salt should be in the forefront of research in its own field. If the Church does not take the initiative in this matter of criticism, its enemies will. This happened in the nineteenth century, and the results were apparent enough: The

Church was discredited, the semieducated masses were shaken in their beliefs, there were painful misunderstandings, blundering condemnations, irretrievable losses of time . . .

A real man of faith must prefer anything to an imposture. May the Church give an example of intellectual courage and no longer hesitate to encourage a rational critique of its tradition. That is what the élite, both of the faithful and of unbelievers, expect of the Church. It is not enough to proclaim the rights of the intelligence; it is necessary to act. As José de Broucker, editor in chief of *Informations Catholiques Internationales*,[5] put it very baldly, "Catholics have said often enough what they had to say; now they must do what they have to do."

[5] This fortnightly review, located at 163 Boulevard Malesherbes, Paris, France, is invaluable for Christians desirous of being intelligently informed about religious developments in France and other parts of the world.

2

The Duty
to be Free

For you have been called to liberty,
brethren.

Galatians 5:13

Where the Spirit of the Lord is, there
is freedom.

2 Corinthians 3:17

Freedom is not a demand presented
by man to God, but a demand presented by God to man. Freedom is
not a right, but a duty.

Nicholas Berdyaev

WITH ALL DUE RESPECT to those who remain more re-
sponsive to the Old Testament than to the New, freedom is really the cornerstone of Christianity. Christ
may be said to have invented and revealed freedom

to men. The "freedom of the glory of the sons of God" is no mirage; it is a mysterious reality experienced by all who live a genuine spiritual life. Christianity is a school of freedom in the highest sense.

Man, the Bible teaches, was created in the image of God; that is, with spirit, intelligence, and freedom. The New Testament began with an interior act of consent—Mary's *fiat*. Christ constantly invites his disciples to achieve deeper personal maturity by spiritual means. Jesus never used coercion; still less did he seek to trap people by means of moral pressure (oh, the horrible blackmail which churchmen sometimes resort to!). God proposes—with overwhelming discretion—and man disposes. The rich young man in the Gospels "went away sad, for he had great possessions," and Jesus did not try to stop him. Yet we know from Mark how much Jesus loved him. Jesus did not impose anything—neither his grace, nor his miracles,[1] nor even his presence. On occasion, he fled to escape honors. Theoretically, and if only to fulfill the longings of his contemporaries, he could have come as a conqueror and could have established himself as a temporal leader; he could

---

[1] "Thou didst not come down from the Cross . . . for again, Thou wouldst not enslave man by a miracle, and didst crave faith given freely, not based on miracle. Thou didst crave for free love and not the base raptures of the slave before the might that has overawed him for ever." (Dostoevsky, *The Brothers Karamazov*, Book V, Chapter V: "The Grand Inquisitor" [New York: The Modern Library], p. 265.)

have been, more exactly, the "liberator" of an enemy-occupied territory. But it was not enough to free men from the oppressor's yoke; he had more and better things to do. By resisting the proposals of the Evil One in the desert, Christ taught men not only to overcome "temptations" but also to preserve their freedom from the aberrations of the spirit of pleasure and domination.

Christ passed through the world, a figure of love and of truth, sometimes tender, sometimes violent, but always just, charitable, and effective. A word, a gesture, a few syllables traced in the sand,[2] a laconic command ("Come, follow me!"), and destinies were changed, souls reborn, hearts filled with joy. Jesus walked on the waters, as though inadvertently; he chatted with Samaritans, prostitutes, and children; he spoke to them of mercy and forgiveness. He used the humblest earthly realities as symbols—well water, the lilies of the field, seeds and fruits, bread and wine, birds and fish. Never did a man speak like this man. He walked beside the disciples as they made their way toward Emmaus in the gathering darkness, mysterious and persuasive, ardent as desire, silent as a promise.

The only pressure he allowed himself to bring to bear on those who drew near him was that of his love, which they were always free to reject. A terri-

[2] These are the only words which Christ is known to have written.

ble power indeed! Jesus met it with only the infinite attraction of his gaze. No one could tell which would prevail—man's weakness or God's strength. The creature can say "no" to his Creator and boast of it. Christ, standing before Dostoevsky's Grand Inquisitor, is silent. His silence reaches an intensity so dramatic as to make of the scene probably the finest piece of writing in all religious literature. This key text should be read in its entirety, since in it all the threads of Dostoevsky's religious dialectics converge. It is like a luminous fresco, portraying the whole destiny of humanity, one part of which falls prey to the obsession of domination, while others batten on collective subjection. The Inquisitor has arrested Jesus in order to put him to death. His argument, in essence, is this: Man is too weak to be allowed to use his freedom. You have been too good to him. That is why you have failed. We, on our part, have corrected your work. Our love for man is more lucid than yours. We have made of men a docile flock in our all-powerful hands. All they have to do is to obey us. The responsibilities weigh on us alone. As for them, they are happy because they are freed from the unendurable burden of their liberty.

Christ listens to this flood of words without speaking; the Inquisitor waits in vain for a reply. This silence oppresses him. All Jesus does is to look deeply into his eyes; then, drawing close to him, he gently kisses the old man's lips. Whereupon the Inquisitor gives up the idea of killing Jesus and lets him out of prison. The kiss burns his heart, but he abides by his theory.

That is the theme of the Legend of the Grand Inquisitor. There is no doubt that Dostoevsky identified socialism and the Catholic Church—of which he knew chiefly the seamy side—with his Grand Inquisitor. But would anyone deny that a most questionable authoritarianism was—and remains, in an attenuated but still vigorous form—the great temptation of the Roman Church?[3] To try to make people happy without their co-operation and even against their will— that is the essential betrayal. Christ's fundamental secret lies in respect for freedom.

Fr. X. Tilliette writes:

The scars it has inflicted on freedom are faults which the Church can never expiate. Influence wrongly used, indiscretion, compromise, violation of conscience, repression of adversaries or unbeleivers—these are blows at the heart of Catholicism. Nevertheless, in the inmost depths of its authentic truth, the Roman Church cannot feel itself wounded by the anathemas of the Legend. For the Church itself condemns these historical

[3] "So they take the cross by the other end and make a sword of it and strike us with it! . . . They take the cross and they turn it around. . . ." From *The Last of the Just*, by André Schwarz-Bart (New York: Atheneum, 1960), p. 324.

aberrations. . . . In reality, the spirit of freedom is
engraved in the smallest iota of dogma and the
most minor point of Catholic morals. . . . Effective
freedom is inalienably imprinted in the whole of
Catholic organization, at its own risk.[4]

Violations of this freedom are the more scandalous
in that they directly conflict with the doctrine taught
by the Church. Catholicism is untrue to the law of
its own being when it violates freedom. Some theologians have indeed sought to justify such errors, but
in vain. No argument, no logic, can shake the evangelical rock on which the Church was founded. In
matters of doctrine, the duty of intolerance has never
outweighed the duty of respecting freedom. We
should blush to have to insist on something so obvious, to have to contrast law and fact, theory and
practice. But contemporary religious ignorance is so
great, and past and present abuses have been so frequent, that it may, perhaps, be useful to recall these
operative principles of Christianity.

The Catholic Church has always and everywhere
taught that the act of faith is a free act. The act has
value only if conscience presents faith as a higher
good than unbelief, and if reason sees no diriment
impediments to it. Conscience remains the highest

---

[4] Cf. *La Légende du Grand Inquisiteur,* preceded by religious
texts selected and translated into French by Cyrille Wilczkowski,
Introduction by X. Tilliette, S.J. (Paris: Desclée de Brouwer.)

tribunal, the court of last resort, whose judgment every self-respecting man must accept. Catholic theology does not merely recognize, it proclaims the inalienable rights of freedom of conscience.[5] To remove this rampart is to undermine the foundations of Christianity, to deny Christ's supreme achievement, to return to pagan barbarism and its tortures. Alas, paganism sweeps the earth unceasingly; in the twentieth century we have known it as Fascism, Nazism, Communism.

St. Thomas Aquinas deals with this major question with his usual clarity and vigor. He maintains that even if the conscience is objectively in error, it always remains the immediate rule of conduct. *Conscientia etiam erronea ligat,* states Canon Law. St. Thomas cites a specific example, which requires no further comment: "To believe in Christ is good in itself, and necessary for salvation; but the will does not tend thereto, except inasmuch as it is proposed by the reason. Consequently, if it be proposed by the reason as something evil, the will tends to it as something evil."[6]

[5] There is some ambiguity in the expression, "freedom of conscience." Sometimes it is linked to a fundamental skepticism, a philosophical indifferentism, a subjectivism, which we are obviously not discussing in these pages. In that sense, it is too far-reaching. It may also be too restrictive if it evokes no more than "tolerance" of religious, philosophical, or political opinions.

[6] *Summa Theologica,* I–II, q. 19, a. 5. Cf. also Fr. Riquet's Lenten sermon preached at Notre Dame in Paris in 1955: "L'Eglise, liberté du monde" (Editions Spes).

What Is Catholicism?

Asked to propose a toast, Cardinal Newman exclaimed, raising his glass: "To the Pope! But first, to conscience!" Why is it that this reservation, engraved on the very heart of Catholicism, should sound almost incongruous? Here we can gauge the sum of prejudices and errors of a great many Catholics, Protestants, and unbelievers concerning the Roman doctrine. The apparent or real repudiation by eccelesiastics of this common teaching of the Church has finally triumphed in the collective mind. This is a scandal which doubtless has many explanations, but it is still inexcusable.

The Church also teaches the supremacy of conscience and the inalienableness of personal responsibility in connection with the virtue of prudence. But who knows what prudence means in the language of the Church?

The virtue of prudence consists in seeking and finding the means suited to the end which a man has set himself. This kind of prudence, therefore, has no relation to timidity. On the contrary, it can call for heroic means if the end proposed requires them. As Mgr. Garrone has put it, prudence is the virtue of highest Christian daring, of true decisions according to Christ, decisions which are always creative audacities and which, in human eyes, often appear as reckless ventures.

But the person who has to choose the means by which he can reach the end he has set himself is really best placed to assess the situation. After he has done whatever he can to enlighten his conscience, he finally comes face to face with himself and has to form a personal opinion. And this no one can do for him, especially if he has great responsibilities.

To rely entirely on another's judgment would be an abdication, perhaps culpable, certainly regrettable. Hence the task of the priest who is somewhat ambiguously referred to as a "spiritual director" (as though a conscience could be directed!) consists essentially in helping his fellow man come to his own decisions, and not in making them for him.[7]

The exercise of freedom of conscience involves an irrevocable solitude. It is said of "leaders" that they are tragically alone. But in a sense, every man has important responsibilities, if only that of living according to his ideal. This solitude of the free man is the price of his greatness. He can relinquish it only at the risk of moral suicide. By becoming no more than an agent who executes the commands of another, a man loses the opportunity of being a creator, in the image of God.

This liberty and this solitude produce something like anguish. To choose, to decide, is a painful act be-

[7] Christians in the Protestant tradition often show more respect than Catholics for the rights of the individual conscience. Frank Buchman, founder of the Moral Rearmament Movement, was described as "simply having faith in what was best in man." Replying to an anguished plea for guidance, he said: "I don't know, but you must find the solution yourself."

cause it requires a leap into the void, because it presupposes that at a given moment a man makes up
his mind to silence his reasons for doubting. "Are
you sure?" asks the scrupulous person in his per-
plexity, seeking reassurance from another. "Are you
sure?" But of course not! That is just the point; one
is never sure of anything, save of the difficulty of
forming a sound opinion. Yet one has to act just the
same, to overcome one's hesitations, and then to
stand firm. As soon as a problem really involves the
interior life, one has to resign himself to not being
sure. Joan of Arc, asked whether she was in a state
of grace, replied: "If I am, may God keep me so; if I
am not, may God place me in it!" Even where human
love is concerned, are we absolutely sure of loving or
of being loved? Ill-considered convictions are proof
of a certain spiritual infantilism. The true saint, the
true philosopher, the true believer, knows that he
does not know. In his old age, Monsieur Pouget, who
had spent his life working, resigned himself to what
he called his "learned ignorance."

To give up one's freedom, to desire to be no more
than a pawn on a chessboard, are not Christian attitudes. Christ came to free man, to raise him above
himself, to confer on him a supernatural dimension
which excludes all mechanical gestures, all passive
compliance, all mediocrity of mind or heart. To be a
Christian means to be prepared to live dangerously,
to blaze new trails alone, to feel one's way in the

semidarkness.[8] It means, ultimately, to put one's trust in him who is more present to us than we are to ourselves, but whom we never see and whose soundless voice we hear only by the practice of patience, humility, and prayer.

In this perspective, we may ask, what becomes of the duty of obedience by which the Catholic Church sets so much store? Is there not some conflict between the duty of obedience and the duty of assuming the burden of personal freedom? Many of our contemporaries believe there is, and they mistakenly set obedience against Christian freedom.

To be free does not mean making up one's own standards from scratch, neither does it mean refusing the necessary commitments toward the civil or religious society to which one belongs. To be free presupposes, on the contrary, that one is linked to something greater than oneself, that one is dependent upon a community. Human liberty, which is not an absolute, is exercised within a system of references which we accept because they appear to us to be true.[9] We are always free to reject one reference

[8] "Freedom is something terribly difficult, it is a burden, it is harsh. . . . Freedom begets suffering. And those who fear suffering repudiate freedom and hand themselves over to authority, to any kind of tyranny." "Freedom is heroic. . . . Freedom is spiritual. . . . Men of servile instinct will never understand what freedom is; they will always slander it." (Unpublished paper of Nicholas Berdyaev, *Le Monde,* March 23, 1952.)

[9] To recognize and accept the obvious, whether in the material or in the spiritual order, is not tantamount to surrendering one's

and to choose another which we think better, but we are definitely bound to choose one. To be free means advisedly accepting one discipline or another. The complete skeptic is ultimately less free than the believer because he does not know in what direction to exercise his freedom. Like the ass in the fable, he is in danger of dying of spiritual starvation between two types of food which he has disdained.

In the same way, obedience does not mean surrendering one's power of decision into the hands of a superior. It means deciding freely, and after mature reflection, to follow this particular leader because one sees in him the embodiment of an authority which one recognizes as necessary, as the depositary of a promise, even if the leader himself is not always competent or infallible. In the Church, the Catholic obeys his bishop or the pope because he believes that they are the historical successors of the Apostles and thus have received from God himself the command to feed his lambs and his sheep. In obeying, the Christian is conforming to the logic of his faith. Obedience, for him, means acting according to his conscience, and hence remaining free.

Christian obedience is not blind obedience on the military pattern.[10] It always remains conditional;

---

freedom and becoming a slave: Two and two make four; Greece is smaller than France; the ethic of the Beatitudes is superior to that of the Decalogue; one must obey God rather than man, etc.

[10] "The duty of loyalty is no excuse for failing in intelligence," states Henri Marrou.

that is, the Christian is in duty bound to disobey if the command received is obviously contrary to faith and morals. When a man believes in conscience that a particular order is seriously detrimental to what he considers to be the welfare of the community for which he is responsible, it is open to him to offer his resignation, and to do so with all the urgency which the gravity of the situation seems to him to require.[11] A worthy superior, whose duty it is to serve the common good, can only be grateful to a subordinate who has the courage to set forth objections to what he considers an unfortunate order and, if necessary, to sacrifice his position in order to prevent some injustice or error.

However, it makes no sense for a Catholic who has faith to separate himself from the Church. The Catholic cannot fail to realize that, by breaking the bonds of ecclesial unity, he is committing an evil action, that he is giving in to pride, and that he is actually preferring himself to God. Henri Marrou put it very well: "No cause, however just, can justify rebellion and schism: unity is so transcendent a good that a Catholic cannot entertain the idea that he, a mere twig, should cut himself off from the rest of the Lord's vine."

[11] The history of the Church records a number of resignations of prelates, which created something of a stir. A case in point was the resignation of Cardinal Billot.

3
The Duty
to Love

Love is affective or it is not love. But
the only kind of affectivity we know
today is that of feeling. We have lost
the sense of spiritual affectivity. The
spirit is love as well as knowledge.

Fr. P. R. Régamey

CAN LOVE BE COMMANDED? Christ was categorical.
His first, last, and sole precept was: "Thou shalt love
the Lord thy God with thy whole heart, and with thy
whole soul, and with thy whole mind. This is the
greatest and the first commandment. And the second
is like it, Thou shalt love thy neighbor as thyself"
(Matthew 22:37–40).

What kind of love is this, then, that it can be imposed as an obligation, the obligation to love God
whom no one has ever seen, a mysterious and distant

reality; the obligation to love one's neighbor, whom we see only too much and whose faults, which are like our own, weary and disgust us?

The difficulty is real if we see in love no more than a spontaneous inclination of the heart, a romantic, violent, narrowly circumscribed sentiment which makes the universe turn around a single being and obscures the sense of kinship with other men.

Is love, in the sense of charity, as Christ commands it, compatible with this form of human love, or is it radically different?

Many Christians believe that charity appeals exclusively to the will, and that it is content with complete absence of feeling. We have all met those pious but inflexible persons, those men and women who "do their duty," those irreproachable practicing Catholics who "love" with a habitual dryness of heart, who force themselves to be helpful, to smile without conviction, to give without enthusiasm of their money, their time, their work.

Are these the Christians Christ desires? We must be careful, of course, not to judge such persons. We do not know what wounds they bear, what efforts they have made, what silent victories they have won over difficult temperaments which incline them, perhaps, to total egotism, melancholy, or despair. Objectively, however, these "charitable" persons are caricatures. The saints, whether canonized or not, are made of different stuff. Evangelical charity, when it has reached its fullness, is recognizable by its effortlessness, its spontaneity, its ease, the joy it radiates. If a man of faith is spiritually well balanced, his goodness, devotion, and inner gaiety seem natural. His qualities are irresistibly attractive. Where love of God or neighbor—even of the most cherished wife—does not lead to a desire for universal communion, to a sort of tenderness for all, and particularly for the most unfortunate, it is a suspect love, an impure compound of egotism and weakness. There is no reason to admire it, or envy it, or present it as a success.

The person who is ever complaining: "I love such a one too much to live far from him, to accept his indifference, or to think of anyone else," is deluding himself. It is rather because he does not love the other enough that his love is an obstacle, that it acts as a screen, that it gnaws at his heart and isolates him. All the mystics—despite their "dark nights" and their difficulties—bear witness to this. Love of God—and even human love if it is genuine—is inseparable from the idea of detachment. Nay more, it prompts a desire for self-sacrifice. "Greater love than this no one has," Christ says, "that one lay down his life for his friends." The man who shies away from sacrifice has not understood the meaning of love.

The love which Christ demands of us is not a cut-rate love, but, on the contrary, a love in full flower, a love of inclination, a purified love. And that is why

Christ could make of love a commandment. For this kind of love requires asceticism. Love which is centered only around pleasure, whether of soul or body, is stillborn and leads to the worst tragedies.

St. Paul calls upon Christians to "rejoice, as though not rejoicing," to "use this world, as though not using it" (1 Corinthians 7:30–31). This does not mean that the Christian must despise the joys of this world and of human love, but that he must not be enslaved by them. That is the price of joy.

The love of God, as such, also requires a kind of detachment. The saint is not so very anxious to die, although he knows that death will bring him closer to God. He wants to live in order to do good and to suffer so as to fulfill what is lacking in the Passion of Christ, as St. Paul so daringly puts it. There is no masochism about such a desire. The Christian does not love suffering for its own sake, but as an instrument of redemption.

This is the detachment—a matter of the will, first, before it reaches the feelings—which Christ demands. Once achieved, the way is open for the heart and the affections. Demonstrative love then comes into its own. Sacrificial love leads to agape, the fervor of purified desire. "The blessed," observes St. Augustine, "do not have what they desire; they desire what they have." The connection between eros and agape, so often denied, could not be better defined.

Christian love is recognizable by its purifying and ennobling effect on its possessor; it does not stifle his sensitivity or feelings. "Stoical" love is no more Christian than a love that degrades. The latter, at best, can be termed an attachment. A love which does not dilate the soul as well as the heart is stamped with mediocrity. The violence of a passion alone is no warrant of its nobility. The greatest love is not the noisiest or the most demonstrative. It is recognizable rather by its discretion, its spiritual fruits, and its stability.

We shall be judged, finally, by love, and by love alone. Intelligence which is not at the service of love is useless, whereas love is sufficient to itself. It is the infallible barometer of our interior life. Faith and hope will pass away; love will not pass away. When he commanded his Apostles to love one another, Christ said explicitly, "By this will all men know that you are my disciples. . . ." Not the gift but the manner of giving touches the heart of the recipient, and at the same time justifies the giver.

In the eyes of those who deny the supernatural dimensions of reality, Christian charity makes exorbitant demands. "Love your enemies," Christ says, "do good to those who hate you, and pray for those who persecute and calumniate you. . . . If you love those that love you, what reward shall you have? . . . Do not even the Gentiles do that?" (Matthew 5:44–47)

There is the touchstone. There we see how few there are who fully deserve the name of Christians. To be a Christian meant, for instance, blessing the Nazi butchers in Dachau; it meant praying for the German N.C.O. who came to call the roll in front of the hutments of the prison camps; it meant loving all the Germans in the midst of the war; a short while back it meant regarding the Algerian rebel as a brother with a right to our respect, however horrible his acts of violence might have been.

Only grace makes a man capable of loving his enemies. Nevertheless, on the purely human level, depth psychology can be of some help. For it helps one to understand others better, to grasp the unconscious motives behind their most odious actions. It explains the causes of certain natural antipathies. It can prevent rash judgments or hasty censure. The Gospel injunction, "Judge not!" turns out to be the attitude most consistent not only with charity but also with truth. What, in any case, could be more realistic than to treat others with the indulgence which we would like for ourselves?

We know today from science that only love can build in lasting fashion. Hate bears absurd fruits; it ravages minds and hearts. On the social level, it leads to armed warfare, which is meaningless since the invention of nuclear weapons. It leads straight to collective suicide.

Love—forgiving others' trespasses, staking on the good in others—can, on the contrary, work miracles.

Moral Rearmament at least has the merit of trying to make people realize that trust, humility, and forgiveness are better than suspicion, pride, and revenge. That does not mean that we should abandon all caution, but, on the contrary, that we should exercise greater lucidity, and dare confront all events squarely so as to draw from them the norms of conduct suited to the circumstances.

St. Louis was a more effective statesman than Machiavelli, and Joan of Arc a better military leader than Hitler. Someday, when passions have cooled, historians will recognize that Pétain, in 1940, and de Gaulle, in 1960, gave proof of political generosity, the former by his readiness to sacrifice his prestige in order to "lessen France's misfortune," and the latter by offering freedom to the French African colonies and to Algeria, despite France's legitimate grounds for retaining them under its control.

We now have scientific proof that racism is erroneous. After two thousand years of Christianity, we have realized that all men are brothers, whatever the color of their skin, and that the theory of masters and slaves has no rational foundation. Psychology, moreover, has shown us that the distance between the most virtuous man and the depraved, the criminal, or the madman, is not as great as we had supposed. The boundary line between good and evil, between psychic balance and disorder, passes through the heart of every man. In each of us there slumbers a coward or a hero, an honorable man or a scoundrel. To love our neighbor as we love ourselves is indeed the most just and the most fruitful attitude.

Ama et fac quod vis,[1] wrote St. Augustine. Love is the highest law, rendering all other laws superfluous. The man who does not love, or who loves less, has no right to pass judgment. Love alone gives knowledge of others. It is passion which blinds. Love is lucid. It makes things transparent. It is the only real bond between beings, between the Creator and his creatures. It alone makes unity possible. It lowers the most insuperable barriers, puts the most dissimilar persons on an equal footing. The Eucharist is the sacrament of unity because it is the sacrament of love. We find the archetype of all love in the bonds which unite the three Persons in God. The Holy Spirit is the divine name of love. Christ came to reveal the Spirit to us, and he left us in order to send us the "Paraclete" who will "renew the face of the earth." Borne on this divine breeze, the Christian goes forth to spread the Good News, that is, to reveal God's love to men and to teach them to love one another in God.

When a mystic wants to speak of divine love, he has no choice but to use the words of human love. The author of the Song of Songs, John of the Cross, Teresa of Avila, Thérèse of Lisieux—all have put the stamp of indefeasible nobility on the expression of the most passionate love. Human love, even the

---

[1] "Love, and do as thou wilt."

humblest and the most debased, is still the symbol and the witness of man's unmitigable desire for an absolute which both transcends him and encompasses him. The restlessness of his heart and of his senses cries out for those who can read the mystery, the immense thirst of man deprived of his ontological unity.

By centering its whole doctrine on love and summing it up in love, Christianity has attained heights which cannot be transcended. The spark which flared in Bethlehem has not ceased to inflame and transfigure the world. Nothing will halt that conflagration. The most marvelous and exciting systems, if they reject this revolutionary love or wrench it out of its supernatural dimension, are doomed to failure. To struggle against Christ, whose kingdom is not of this world, is hopeless. St. Paul's paean will resound until the end of time like a shout of triumph and of truth: ". . . if I have all faith so as to remove mountains, yet do not have charity, I am nothing. And if I distribute all my goods to feed the poor, and if I deliver my body to be burned, yet do not have charity, it profits me nothing. Charity is patient, is kind; charity does not envy, is not pretentious, is not puffed up, is not ambitious, is not self-seeking, is not provoked; thinks no evil, does not rejoice over wickedness, but rejoices with the truth; bears with all things, believes all things, hopes all things, endures all things. Charity never fails . . ." (1 Corinthians, 13:3–8)

4
God — What For?

Of two men who do not have the experience of God, the man who denies him is perhaps the closer to him.

Simone Weil

"IF GOD created man in his own image, man has certainly paid him back in kind!" Thus Voltaire, who had some grounds for attacking the Catholics of his time. In this respect, things have not changed much since the eighteenth century.

Some Catholics make a habit of speaking of God with an obnoxious familiarity. They have made of him a creation of their minds, in the image of our mediocrity. The caricatures of God are without number, and they help to turn unbelievers away from a religion which, in practice, tolerates deplorable distortions. Because they go to church and receive the sacraments, many Catholics think they can speak of

God as they please, as of someone whose every secret they know and whose every reaction they can
guess.

For some, God is a sort of top sergeant or police-
man, especially interested in ferreting out offenders;
a niggling bookkeeper who enters our good and bad
deeds in his ledger; a choleric schoolmaster weary
of men's infidelities and always ready to mete out
punishment; an unbending customs officer whom we
had better obey, because he knows everything and
can do anything.

For others, God is an implacable judge whose fa-
vorite weapon is "immanent justice." I once knew a
healer, a fervent Catholic, who maintained that every time the father of a family was unfaithful to his
wife, God took vengeance by permitting the death
of one of his children.

For more sophisticated believers, God is the great
"clockmaker" who perfected the whole machinery of
the universe once and for all at the moment of creation, and since then has no care for it, since it works
on its own. He is a distant, inaccessible God, indifferent to men's sufferings, who does not need our
prayers and lamentations, for the wheel of destiny is
inexorable and blind, crushing innocent and guilty
alike.

For still others, God is a sort of all-powerful fairy
whose magic wand can, on occasion, transform hand-
kerchiefs into white mice or carriages into pumpkins;

a magician who makes statues weep or bleed, who liquefies the blood of St. Januarius on fixed dates, who starts or stops epidemics, repairs broken bones, or causes the absent-minded driver to step out of his smashed automobile unscathed[1]

This is the God of every kind of magic, who scoffs at the laws of nature, of which he is nevertheless the author. He is the God who listens to our most preposterous requests, who, for instance, makes the dunce pass his examinations because his grandmother lit a candle. He is the benevolent despot, accessible to all requests, provided one pays his price; the God of cheap miracles who soothes toothache and helps the cow to calve; the God of Ouija boards, ghosts, bilocation, and all the miraculous trumpery which sends shivers down the backs of the gullible.

There is also the amulet God, who will grant a "good death" to the wearer of a medal or scapular; the God of bankers, the God of Pharisees, the God

[1] This is not to make light of the evangelical concept of providence, or to cast doubt upon it. "The very hairs of your head are all numbered," Jesus said. The Christian God constantly watches over his children; he knows each one by name, like the good shepherd. But there is an infantile way of conceiving of the action of providence. We must be honest. If we think that God is responsible for the happy events of our lives, that it is he, for example, who saves the reckless driver who hits a tree at eighty miles an hour, then he is also responsible for the disasters which befall us. There cannot be two yardsticks.

Our conception of God is surely very childish if we believe that he intervenes directly to change the laws of nature. Providence is the certainty that God, who sees all and has created everything, knows what happens to us, and unceasingly offers us his grace.

of "well-bred people," the middle-class God who listens only to the prayers of distinguished persons who make large contributions, the God of gilded marble ex-votos.

There is the cruel, sadistic God who consigns to hell the poor wretch who refuses to observe the Friday abstinence—as well as the unbaptized savage in the bush. Not so long ago, missionaries were still being taught that they were going to snatch the heathen from the jaws of hell.

There is the "makeshift" God who is declared responsible for natural phenomena when scientists cannot discover their cause (for example, spontaneous generation).

Finally there is the God of the imbeciles, evoked by Simone de Beauvoir in her *Memoirs*: "Perhaps God himself was as fussy and narrow-minded as a religious bigot; perhaps God was stupid."[2] To which François Mauriac had already replied: "Only imbeciles would claim that God preferred imbeciles!"

In religious congregations of women, one can find teaching nuns who pity the "lonely" Jesus, the "divine prisoner" of the tabernacle. The Real Presence has sometimes been a pretext for the worst disorders of the senses: bleeding Hosts, Hosts which rise into the air by their own power or refuse to stay on the tongue of the sinner.

The unbeliever with an innate respect for the sa-

[2] *Memoirs of a Dutiful Daughter* (Cleveland and New York: The World Publishing Company, 1959), p. 143.

cred utterly rejects such stupidities, frauds, and corruptions, just as does the intelligent believer. Can we tell how many persons of good will, suffering from the effects of an inept religious education or the pettiness of their elders in the "faith," have turned away from a God so distorted by the very persons whose responsibility it was to reveal him to them? And what shall we say of the harm done by some Catholic schools in which students of weaker moral fiber have been deformed for life by the counterfeit coin dealt out to them year after year? Who can say how many of the young men and women today were exposed as youngsters to the concerted inanities of their teachers and families, and gave up all religious practice for want of meeting an intelligent priest or teacher at the right time?

The "bad example" of unbelievers, the "lacunae" in public-school programs, the sectarianism of certain teachers—these are all very easy to blame. But let the Catholic who thinks that he has never given scandal himself throw the first stone!

Christians, even the most clear-sighted, have been too slow in pointing to the irreparable harm caused to young and defenseless minds by certain methods of so-called "Christian" education. And it is only too true that a loss of the sense of the sacred, religious indifference, or even a most aggressive atheism have often been signs of a healthy reaction. There are atheists whose intellectual probity and moral rectitude bear witness to God, in that they have rejected the caricatures offered to them as true images of divinity. "Certain forms of atheism," writes Fr. Liégé, "should be read as an indictment of infantile expressions of the faith."[3]

"The terrifying phenomenon of atheism," declares Hans Urs von Balthasar, "might be, among other things, a dispensation of providence designed to force mankind, and especially the Christian world, to return to a higher conception of God."[4]

Jean Lacroix, the Catholic philosopher, writes on the same subject: "The reason why I am so grateful to my atheist friends is that they have taught me not to cheat. . . . The greatest merit of present-day atheism is that it has undertaken a tremendous intellectual debunking operation by challenging all idolatry."[5]

After indulging in a rather clumsy distinction between the God of the Christians and the God of the philosophers and scientists, we are now reaching a point where we shall stress the similarities rather than the differences. Fortunately! Otherwise there would be two truths, which would amount to an admission that there was none. Philosophers, theolo-

---

[3] *Adultes dans le Christ* (Brussels: Pensée Catholique), p. 28.

[4] *Science, Religion, and Philosophy* (Westminster, Md.: Newman Press, 1958).

[5] *Le sens de l'athéisme moderne* (Casterman). Jean Guitton, for his part, says: "Basically, man is idolatrous or iconoclastic; he is not atheistic" (*L'Eglise et l'Evangile* [Paris: Grasset]).

gians, and scientists need all the light their combined disciplines can shed to form an acceptable idea of God. The philosopher has not had to invent God, but only to take stock of the God presented by religion; reflection on God is fruitful only if it is applied to something other than one's own fancies. The twentieth century no longer has any desire to set the God of Abraham, Isaac, and Jacob over against the God of the philosophers, for the same reason that it no longer regards it necessary to set science and philosophy over against faith. It sees in them approaches to God, autonomous, irreducible, but complementary.

How are we to speak of God without sounding absurd, like the "right-thinking" people, or presumptuous, like the pseudo-theologians? In the first place, by realizing—in line with the Bible, the mainstream of the Church's tradition, and the greatest "doctors" of the Church—that God is beyond all concept. Strictly speaking, God is unknowable: "No man has ever seen God, for he would die."

It is impossible, really, to speak of God otherwise than by analogy. "I am quite sure," wrote Simone Weil, "that there is not a God in the sense that I am quite sure nothing real can be anything like what I conceive when I pronounce this word."[6]

While it is relatively easy to speak of God nega-

[6] *Gravity and Grace* (New York: G. P. Putnam's Sons, 1952), p. 167.

tively, by saying what he is not, it is very much harder to speak of him positively. Even the believer —especially the believer—who calmly asserts that there are three "persons" in God ought to recall that he is speaking by analogy, and at once add that God is "suprapersonal." No notion of our experience can, without amendment, be appropriate to God. "God alone speaks rightly about God," as Pascal said.

Jean Lacroix is justified in thinking that "the time has no doubt come to put more emphasis on the unbelief of the believer." It is indeed a matter of emphasis, for in its doctrine the Church has always held that God eludes all categories and any complete comprehension by the human intellect. The Church maintains that the human reason can arrive at the conclusion that God exists, but it has never claimed that God could be known in the mystery of his being —even with the assistance of Revelation. The dogma of the Trinity, which, in the eyes of the faithful, contains the most profound truths that man is able to stammer about God, is a mystery. God defies all definition. If man's intelligence leads to God—and that is the only way it can avoid absurdity—it will always come up against the mystery of this "superbeing."[7] Our human language will never penetrate that mystery. Skepticism comes back into its own at the end of even the very best of rational roads to God. Every

[7] The expression has now become accepted because of its use by Fr. Sertillanges.

intellectual and sensible representation of God is inadequate, because the finite, the relative, cannot "express" the infinite and the absolute. This is so obvious that it is unfortunately very rarely said. With the result that in practice it is forgotten. Has the generality of believers ever known it? Preachers and catechists are so obsessed with the desire to reassure people that they avoid speaking of these matters, which are nonetheless fundamental. For the most part, intellectual humility is not the strong point of those whose mission it is to preach God and the Gospel. They dispose of the arguments of the unbeliever, but fail to point to the limits of dogmatic representations. Today we are reaping the fruits of this failure. Too many of our contemporaries have turned away from God because of the inadequacies in the representations which were offered to them under the guise of Gospel truth.

This paradox of Valéry's seems to us more fruitful than the blusterings of second-rate apologists: "It is most unfortunate that the Church, which has embraced and assimilated so much, has been unable to absorb unbelievers, those great champions and confessors of the mind."[8]

It would be well if more Catholic writers were to pay tribute to unbelievers. For most of the time it is the unbelievers whose intellectual demands push back the frontiers of the mind and impel the faithful

[8] Paul Valéry, *Lettres à quelques-uns* (Gallimard).

to raise and to cleanse their religious sights. Those who contradict are really the only valuable associates; it is from discussion with them that light emerges.

If God may be defined as the "prime mover," or the "first cause," he cannot be included in a series along with the second causes.[9] The God of the Bible is the Creator, but his creation, which is finite, is not on a level with the Creator, who is infinite. That is why God can never be likened to a watchmaker, or an inventor, or a technician who produces objects, or a human being who begets another human being, in every way like unto himself. There is a vertiginous chasm between the Author and his work. The Church, with the Protestant tendency amputated, has sufficiently emphasized the resemblance between man and God, and not enough, perhaps, the difference. And Karl Barth may be pardoned for stating that the doctrine of analogy of being constitutes, in his view, the only valid reason for not becoming a Catholic.

God is the principle, the source, the foundation. As Jean Lacroix says: "God, for man, is not an object, but an Absolute for which there is an exigency in the heart of the subject. To admit of God is not to admit of a given, but of a giver; it is not to presume

[9] "Plotinus," writes Henry Duméry, "called God 'the One,' only because he had no word for 'zero'" (cf. some mystics who have referred to God as "nothingness" or "nothing").

that the problem is solved, but to work toward a solution capable of being produced; it is not to believe
that the true and the good are ready-made, but that
one can and must create them. The One, Plotinus
said, is not so much an object of the mind, as that
which causes the mind to have objects."[10]

Viewed in this light, at the level which is his own,
God no longer appears as constantly active, in the
manner of an officer in a dugout who has to do everything himself because most of his subordinates
have been wounded or killed. God is not the "doer,"
but "he who is"—the definition is in the Bible—he
who causes others to act. What more childish image
of God than that of a boss constantly meddling in
the works? We shall return to this in connection with
miracles.

"The prestige of the Creator is not heightened by
calling on the prime mover for help every time there
appears to be a temporary breakdown in the secondary causes," writes Hans Urs von Balthasar.[11] The
scientific approach could arise and develop only in
proportion as man realized that nature possessed
enough potentialities to produce of itself results formerly attributed mistakenly to the direct action of
God.

With regard to the appearance of life on earth and
the possibility of "manufacturing" living beings from

[10] Jean Lacroix, *op. cit.*, p. 63.
[11] *Op. cit.*, p. 189.

inorganic matter, Fr. Carles writes: "We do not see why the Church should take offense at this achievement, unless we concede, with the Greeks, that life is a private preserve, an area which God more or less arbitrarily reserves for himself to buttress his shaky authority."[12]

Everything indicates that God is becoming increasingly unnecessary as an explanation of what formerly was inexplicable. This surely signifies that a very false idea of God and of his ways was current. Under the aegis of science, we are witnessing a real purification of the idea of God.[13] We must be glad of this service which science renders religion. The tables have justly been turned. Let us hope that Catholic popularizers will seriously set about the important task of making the faithful realize that crediting man with a thing does not mean discrediting God.

But although God is the unknowable, and although he acts through the natural causes of which he is the author, we should not forget that Jesus is the principal character, so to speak, of Christianity. And in philosophizing too much about the nature of God, we are quite likely to forget it. If Christ is God, he is

[12] *Cahiers d'études biologiques, Origine de la vie sur la terre* (Paris: Lethielleux, 1957).

[13] "Science has indeed killed God," observes Étienne Borne in his book *Dieu n'est pas mort*, "but that God is the pagan God of nature. . . . His downfall began with Genesis and the Gospel, and it has since been abetted, in no small measure, by modern science."

93

also, and no less, Man—that is the irreducible originality of his being. This is the center of the mystery of the Incarnation. Visible, tangible, subject to birth and death, then mysteriously risen, the God-Man "dwelt among us." He is the Emmanuel of the Bible.

Immediately all previous viewpoints are reversed. God, through Christ with whom he is identical, is accessible to us, present in history with a presence capable of being recorded. Unbelievers can challenge this faith in Christ's divinity; they cannot fail to recognize its overwhelming significance and its inexhaustible fecundity. "Let the earth . . . bud forth a Saviour!" writes Isaia. Faced with this ineffable presence, one can only deny, or else adore and give thanks. The dogma of the Incarnation is marvelously in tune with contemporary psychology; it exalts man to the point of "deifying" him. We shall return to this.

But human reflection cannot elude the problems posed by the existence of God. These problems are polarized in what the philosophers call "immanence" and "transcendence."

Immanence means that God is present in the world he created. God, acting through natural causes, unceasingly sustains a world which is in daily process of formation, preserving it from the abyss of nothingness. In him and through him all things have their being. This ontological presence of God at the heart of all being attains its crowning glory in the spiritual being whom God inhabits by his grace, to the extent that man is faithful to his conscience. This is the mystical presence of God in man, which has been intensely experienced by the saints. So much so that one of them, Paul of Tarsus, could say: "It is now no longer I that live, but Christ lives in me" (Galatians 2:20).

Transcendence means that God cannot be identified with the world which he inhabits. Like a surging river, he overflows all the apparent "content" which conceals him, shelters him, and reveals him. God is present in matter, present and active in creation, but he cannot be identified with creation. Science will remind those who might forget this that God can never be caught red-handed, so to speak, acting in nature.

That is why, for want of a better word, we say that God is "supernatural," that is, that he is both in and above nature, both intrinsic and extrinsic to it.

What is difficult is to grasp both poles simultaneously; not to abandon transcendence in favor of immanence (the pantheist temptation), or immanence in favor of transcendence (a more or less Cartesian idealism). God is not a clear idea, as we have already shown. To reduce him to only one of these criteria is to improverish him—in a sense to destroy him. God is not simply the supreme clockmaker *or* "creative evolution." He is both. This is the place, if ever there was one, to repeat Lyautey's golden maxim: "Most mistakes come of using the conjunction 'or' instead of the conjunction 'and.'"

In point of fact, Catholic doctrine has always taken

both these contradictory criteria into account. It has always insisted that the supreme being is both supernatural and intimately related to the world. Here we face the "asses' bridge" of philosophical reflection on God. The extraordinary ingenuity of Catholic thought consists in this, that it affirms both the transcendence and the immanence of God. This refusal to choose between one or the other is a consequence of the Incarnation; Christ is God *and* Man; his nature is both human *and* divine. The mysterious personality of Jesus is the best indication that God is both within and without, interior and exterior; that he is at once presence and absence, wealth and poverty, multiplicity and unity. God is the crossroads and, as it were, the keystone of all contradictions. To reject these contradictions is, in a sense, to refuse to think. One of Christianity's glories is that it has constantly stimulated metaphysical speculation. To rid Western thought of Christianity or monotheistic strivings would be to deal it a mortal blow.

God, like truth, is tension between two opposite poles. Science is right in wanting to get along without God, in wanting to render him unnecessary. Scientific materialism is an excellent working method. The scientist, if he wants to advance, must act as though God did not exist, for he will never find God at the end of his scalpel or under his microscope. As for the philosophers and theologians, they retain their freedom to pursue their speculation beyond the world of appearances and to suspend that world by the golden thread of metaphysics and faith.

Science and philosophy cannot do much against God. But they can help, by their experimental investigations of their critical approach, to purify and clarify his image. Following the scientific crisis of the nineteenth century, our era is rediscovering the legitimacy of spiritual and rational approaches to God. Philosophical atheism is doubtless only a phase in the history of thought, a period of growing pains which man must endure if he is once more to find his proper place in the hierarchy of beings.

We have reached the end of a long tunnel in the history of religious thought. The God of the twenty-first century will be all the more dazzling for that.

5

Faith and
Its Caricatures

> It is in the impoverishment of the
> faith that we must look for the deep-
> est cause of all errors.
> Doctrinal Report of the Plenary
> Assembly of the French Episcopate

"YOU'RE LUCKY—you have your faith . . ." "I don't go to church any more, but I still have my faith . . ." "I lost my faith when my child died . . ." Commonplace or moving phrases—what lies behind those poor words? What ignorance, what good will, what secret anguish do they conceal?

People often speak of the faith as of something they possess, or now only partly possess, like a glove one has mislaid (and what could be more useless than a single glove lying in a drawer?), or an object one picks up or puts down at will, or again, like a name that has slipped one's memory and comes back when least expected.

"To have" faith. On close examination, the expression is faulty. Faith is not in the category of "having" but of "being." One does not "have" faith; one "is" or "is not" a man of faith. One is a man of little or much faith. Faith is a state of mind, a mode of the heart (in Pascal's sense of the word). It is not an illness one contracts, for no apparent reason, and from which one recovers, goodness knows how. It is neither a quality nor a defect. It is not something one inherits, like the family furniture. It is not found in the cradle, or behind the pillar of a cathedral, or even in the baptismal font. It is faith that "has" the believer, that keeps him, to which he belongs. Faith is not a tool. Faith commands, calls, holds one back— like love, which would not be encountered were it not already found.

Faith is not, as is often thought, mere intellectual adherence given once and for all to a system of concepts and values neatly filed away in a card index. Nor is faith a masterly piece of architecture, a wondrous edifice which will crumble to dust if a single stone is removed.

Faith is born, grows, fades, disappears, like daylight or like a fragile plant. It is cared for, tended, neglected, killed; resuscitated on occasion, according as one is an exacting spiritual being, or weak and carnal.

Faith *is* the life of the soul. In faith, man confronts his spiritual destiny. Woe to the man who decides that X has no faith, that Y has lost his faith![1] It is foolish to think faith can be exhaustively defined, its contents inventoried like a library. It is foolhardy to seek to monopolize faith, to trace its visible frontiers, beyond which there can be only shadows.

The Church certainly has the right and the duty to point out the axes along which faith passes; to establish the landmarks whereby one can find one's way and enter into dialogue with others. The Catholic creed enumerates the principal "articles" of faith. It cannot be otherwise. The Church is incarnated in a visible society; it has a body. It has evolved in time and space, grown and suffered in every region of human habitation. This is not, as idealists believe, a necessary evil. It is a good willed by the Church's founder, himself made of flesh and blood, with a history, a genealogy; whose footsteps marked a particular soil; who sailed on a particular lake, identifiable on a map; who rested his head on the deck of a boat.

But let there be no mistake. We can know the catechism by heart, and study theological treatises in every library in the world; we can sing the credo from the illuminated choir lofts of the most beautiful or the ugliest basilicas, but we will never know

[1] Can a person know for sure that he has "lost" his faith? Not unless he has really understood what commitments of mind and heart faith entails. In most cases, "losing one's faith" means giving up a system of infantile values, a pawnshop of dusty beliefs.

the exact, strict meaning to be attached to the "articles" of our faith. For the sole reason, which the Church has proclaimed for twenty centuries—has it been preaching in the wilderness?—that the truths of the faith are mysteries, and that by definition a mystery outranges the capacities of the human intellect.

"Mystery"—we hardly even realize it—is the Christian form of agnosticism. For there is a Christian agnosticism. It means that while we can mark the fluid frontiers of a mystery, we shall never know exactly what merchandise, if we may be permitted to use that vulgar word, is covered by the definition of the mystery.

Orthodoxy, too, is an obscure concept. It has always been defined negatively, in relation to heresies, but its content can never be exhaustively defined. Behind the clear terms of a declaration of faith, there is the abyss of the unknowable. Theology tries, justifiably and often successfully, to define the truths of the faith more and more accurately. But the depths elude it, because the things of God surpass our understanding, and because everything is seen as "through a glass, darkly."

It is an obtuse man who thinks he has God's blueprint in his pocket, who always "brandishes God like a weapon," to quote Monsieur Pouget. He has lost the sense of God, the sense of the Church. He is an impostor, if not a fool.

The Church has defined its dogmas, constructed its

theology—or rather, its theologies—like a cathedral, stone by stone. There is a history of dogma just as there is a history of theology and of human thought. The tree of dogma grows richer from age to age. Why?

Because reason is the "daughter of God," and the religious man could not neglect to ponder the content of the Bible and the tradition of the Church since its inception, without failing in his duty to multiply the talents he has received. This labor of the intellect is one of the finest and most important ever undertaken by man. Only the ignorant can smile at this patient, stubborn effort, which will continue as long as men have living faith.

The Roman Church, historically linked to the primitive Church (the proof lies not in arguments but in facts and documents), has been entrusted with the formidable task of preserving intact the deposit of revealed truth. And with the jealousy of a mother, it guards Revelation against all who would impair its balance or negate its conflicting tensions. It is constantly engaged in purifying doctrine, and regards itself as alone qualified to do so—rather as the lineal descendant of an ancient family considers that he alone is entitled to defend his name and patrimony against rival and unauthorized claims.

That is the logic of the Church. One can accept it or reject it, but one cannot blame the Church for doing what it was created to do. One may regret that it has taken a particular stand, or judge that some other position which it has rejected is preferable, but one cannot deny it the absolute, unconditional right to judge, to condemn, to approve, and to impose obedience by spiritual means. The Catholic Church, whose unity is sometimes so much admired, would be a fairground if a supreme tribunal was not empowered to adjudicate clearly and have its decisions carried out.

Nevertheless, the elaboration of dogma raises difficult problems, especially for our contemporaries, who are so little and so poorly informed about the internal history of Christian thought.

The Church, if it is to speak and to teach—and that is what it was made for ("Go into the whole world and preach the gospel to every creature": Mark 16:15)—is obliged, like everyone else, to use a particular language, which did not fall from heaven, and a philosophical system perfected by men. Had Jesus been born in Japan, he would have spoken Japanese. He was born in the Near East, and spoke Aramaic. Had the Papal See been in Shanghai, the Church Fathers would have used Chinese concepts. The popes were bishops of Rome, and therefore used Western concepts. They had no choice. Nascent Christianity drew on the philosophical strains of Judaism and the Greco-Latin heritage. That is why the formulations of dogma, the propositions of faith, are marked with the stamp of their age and of the culture in which they first saw the light of day. For instance, the divine trilogy of the Scriptures (Father, Son, and Holy Spirit) was meditated and expressed in terms of Western concepts of "nature," "person," "substance," and so on. The same is true of the mysteries of the Incarnation, the Redemption, the Eucharist, and all the other dogmas, including the two most recently defined: the Immaculate Conception and the Assumption.

Will the day come when these great mysteries of the Catholic faith ("Catholic" meaning "universal") are differently expressed in terms of a different philosophical system, in other theologies born in the Far East or in Africa? Let us hope so, for the sake of a universal understanding of the truths of the faith, and of the youthfulness of the Church. If such transformations take place, it will be gradually, without shocks, without breaks with the past, and under the sole control of the successors of the Apostles.[2]

For lack of adequate religious knowledge, the faithful—and a fortiori those outside the Church—are generally unaware of these possibilities.

Thus it is forgotten that the Church is not exempt

[2] It should be noted that faith can be expressed only in terms of concepts, symbols, images. Concepts, symbols, and images may one day be found which reflect the mentality of other times, present and to come, but that would simply mean exchanging one set of expressions for another. It is illusory to think that one can express faith without these intermediaries. Thinking, here, means transposing.

from the laws of growth and development governing any institution. The fact that the Church clarifies a truth which was revealed once for all at a privileged moment of history does not prevent it from looking around and ahead and adapting itself. Its slowness may be deplored. But the day will surely come when a second St. Thomas will elaborate a new synthesis which takes account of the advances of modern thought and science.

These considerations throw some light on the relative and destructible character of the garments of the faith, without, of course, assailing the immutable character of the truths formulated in the dogmas.

But it is also necessary to be quite clear about the relative importance of the various dogmas. Some are at the center of the Christian economy, such as the Trinity, the Incarnation, the Resurrection; others are at the periphery. As Cardinal Lefebvre put it in his doctrinal report of 1957, "[The faithful suffer from] a lack of loftiness of vision and a broad picture of dogma," based on a true "hierarchy of values." For the faithful to be so ill-informed, the priests must have been very inadequate too. Do they not sometimes give equal importance to the content of faith, to its dogmatic expression, to moral theology and its innumerable ramifications, and to the reversible decrees of the Church's magisterium concerning discipline and Canon Law?

Rational formulations of the mysteries are means,

not ends. They have value by reason of their aim. They are windows opening on the divine plan and on the religious significance of creation. Faith must not be confused with the system or systems which give it expression. Nothing is less systematic than the spirit. The creed is not a system. Systems make their appearance only in theology;[3] and there are several theologies whose validity the Church recognizes, although Thomism holds a privileged position because of its exceptional balance.

Our contemporaries, with their deep-seated distrust of systems—of which we can be glad, for it is evidence of a keen sense of the complexity of reality—are not required by the Church to subscribe to one system or another. Here we are in the realm of counsel, not of precept. Faith remains, but systems pass. The Church is no more wedded to a system than to a civilization. A thousand indications, alas, would seem to prove the contrary. But a thousand indications do not constitute a single reality. To realize this, we must go to the true sources, and not take as

[3] The Gospel contains no system. Christ taught by means of parables, symbols, and images which the simple people he was addressing would understand. Was this teaching impaired by its lack of intellectual precision? "Images and symbols are less inadequate as expressions than are intellectual interpretations," wrote Charles Baudouin. "The symbol is given first, as what might be called a biological reality, and its translation into rational concepts comes only later, and remains an inevitable impoverishment" (to "inevitable" we might add, "and indispensable"). "As always when confronted with essentials, poetry is more faithful than prose."

"Nothing is truer than a myth," said Maryse Choisy.

What Is Catholicism?

Gospel truth whatever happens to be said in a village pulpit or set down in third-hand works. Religious literature, which is so rich in remarkable works, is even richer in books of a painful mediocrity, comparable to the knickknacks sold on pilgrimages, in which Huysmans saw Satan's revenge.

Another benefit of genuine faith is that it delivers one from idols, from taboos—in other words, from the constant temptation to shift the weight of the absolute onto human and ephemeral values, onto persons, onto systems. Faith puts everything in its place. It helps to free human beliefs of myths, and to preserve their properly relative character. The man of faith refuses to let himself be carried away by ill-placed passions, for reasons of minor importance. Faith delivers man from the bondage which is sometimes the lot of unbelievers, who seek to quench their thirst for the absolute with ersatz ideals.

The cult of a philosophical system is itself an error which the theologian does not always avoid. One cannot be too careful about asserting that this or that philosophy is incompatible with the faith. Basically, could not faith adapt itself to any "open" philosophy?

We might quote Fr. Henry in this connection: "This absolute, transcendent faith which the Church transmits by word and by the sacraments can be the more liberal . . . to the extent that it is more sure of itself, that is, more conscious of what it has received for the salvation and happiness of the human race."[4]

[4] *Informations Catholiques Internationales,* October 10, 1953.

Faith overcomes ignorance without eliminating it. It is undoubtedly the most precious of lights for the intelligence and a marvelous nourishment for the heart, but it removes neither difficulties nor anxiety. It comes up against the problem of evil or the problem of creation, for instance, without resolving them.

Not only does faith not resolve all problems, but it also creates new ones, if for no other reason than that it broadens the field of our investigations and our curiosity. Only for lazy minds does faith mean security. Faith is a breach in our prison wall which allows new light to filter in. It is not a master key which opens every door. It is the humble certainty that a key must exist and that it will fall into our hands, which will be trembling with joy, when all is consummated.

And yet faith is truly the state of grace of the intelligence. Maximum faith coincides with maximum understanding of the universe of things visible and invisible. And it is accompanied by a maximum of interior joy and peace. Man's heart burns more intensely the closer he draws to God. In a sense, the mystic is the most clear-sighted of men, even if he is uneducated, as was the Curé d'Ars. The intuitions of faith make up to some degree for lack of learning. The lives of the saints make this abundantly clear. The saint is the most effective of all human beings.

Faith cannot be isolated from hope and love. These three theological virtues are interdependent. Without charity, faith is dead. With charity, on the other hand, it causes all the faculties to flourish. Faith is, in a way, a test of spiritual health and vitality. Not that the unbeliever is subjectively diminished because he does not believe. His religious disbelief is to some extent compensated for by other certainties. Every man has his creed. But the genuine man of faith is recognizable by the inimitable ease and effectiveness which he brings to everyday living. Faith, the Gospel tells us, can move mountains. That is, it overcomes practical difficulties which appear insurmountable. It makes everything possible. The man who lives in the intimacy of Christ goes through life like a child at play.[5] Realism and mysticism—Bergson saw it clearly—go hand in hand. The man of God passes through our midst like a lamp bearer. With a smile, a silence, a word, he unravels, soothes, heals.

[5] Mgr. John J. Wright, Bishop of Pittsburgh, suggests that, aside from faith, a sense of humor is the best antidote to the excessive seriousness which often marks our actions.

6

Toward a Better
Understanding of Dogma

> An adult faith presupposes that one
> has interiorized the mystery and
> penetrated the reality expressed in
> the dogmatic formulas.
>
> Fr. Liégé

OWING TO their exclusive preoccupation with scientific objectivity, our contemporaries have lost the habit of considering beings, events, or things in the context of their meaning. When science was in its infancy, it was useful to rid it of dubious subjective considerations so that it might reach universally applicable truths. Mathematical science being the most abstract, it is also the most "exact" of all disciplines; it is the ideal toward which all the others strive.

But this abstraction is not without danger where the humanities are concerned. The historian, for instance, who refuses to express a value judgment about events, impoverishes his work.[1] The same applies, a fortiori, to the psychologist concerned exclusively with sociology—the case is not imaginary—or to the moralist intent on being only a biologist. The chemist is entitled to define water as a compound of hydrogen and oxygen, provided he does not imply that this definition is exhaustive; the physicist, the geologist, the philosopher, the poet, even the theologian, are entitled to offer other definitions of water which will be just as valid in their own spheres.

An unfortunate tendency exists in our times to forget that there are other kinds of knowledge besides scientific knowledge. This is understandable in view of the heady progress achieved in this field and of the technical applications to which it has led, but it is replete with danger. Owing to the prevailing low level of culture, modern man is tempted to think that statements only of a scientific nature are true. Perhaps, in some more or less distant future, by virtue of the pendular movement of thought, "science" will recover a broader meaning than it has had since the nineteenth century. Teilhard de Chardin and his disciples have tried to break down the walls of separation between philosophy, theology, and science. We know, however, what violent opposition this has provoked. Our age is so obsessed with specialization

---

[1] "If only that which is universally verifiable is regarded as historical," writes Fr. Jean Steinmann, "then apparitions do not belong to history."

that it is losing all appreciation of, or taste for, synthesis.

Religion, too, has been affected by this concern with objectivity. We are still suffering the consequences of the Counter Reformation, with its attempt to contain the flood of Protestant subjectivism and relativism. We have only to glance at an elementary textbook of theology. What we find, for the most part, is an abstract construction, a bloodless scholasticism, opening the doors upon a universe which may be very logical and coherent, but which is terribly artificial. Instead of life, spirituality, mysticism, we find an arid and desiccating system. It may be argued that this is not the theologian's business, that there are excellent books of spirituality, and—to each his trade. It is an argument. But, in the first place, few Christians would have the idea of looking elsewhere for more substantial nourishment. And secondly, it is very debatable that the theologian's primary and ultimate task is not the enrichment of the interior life. That, in any case, was how the early Church Fathers saw it—St. Augustine, St. Leo, St. John Chrysostom, and the like.

Particularly since the Renaissance, the Church has not stressed the primacy of life over ideas in religious education. As a result, Catholicism appears in a form which may, perhaps, satisfy the exigencies of pure reason, but which is absolutely unadapted to the needs of the faithful. This is a serious defect, whatever the other merits of classical theology. Crammed with abstractions, syllogisms, and unreal concepts, cut off from the fruits of historical and psychological research, all too many priests have lost the ability— unless they make a great personal effort for which they do not always have the time or inclination—to present the great themes of religion in a living and concrete form.

Take, for instance, a sermon on the Trinity at a Sunday Mass. Ten to one, the priest will have prepared it with the help of a theology manual from his seminary days. He will give a lecture on the three Persons in God, on the unity of the divine essence, on the relations between Father, Word, and Spirit, on the "processions," "divine missions," etc. At best, the average Catholic will perhaps admire the speculative skill of the theologians, but he will speedily forget all these considerations, which have no apparent bearing on his life.

Yet the sermon could have been vitalized by a few quotations from the Old and New Testaments, as well as by some account of the origin of the doctrine and its place in the history of the Church and in the spirituality of the saints. The doctrine of the Trinity derives directly from the Scriptures; only subsequently was it elaborated in philosophical terms to combat heretical tendencies. It gives the believer a vision of the living God present in his soul through grace. The trinitarian life, prototype of the life of men in community, is of interest to the individual only if it is offered to him as a nourishment of the soul.[2] The merciful fatherhood of God, the incarnation of the Son, who is both mediator and shepherd, the power of the Spirit who "inspires" the intelligence by his gifts and communicates his love—these are so many royal roads by which to approach the divine mystery. Outside this context, the virtuosities of the theologians are but "tinkling cymbals."[3]

Not so long ago, Pope Pius XII proclaimed the dogma of the Assumption. Some of the bishops whom the Pope had called upon to give their views on the advisability of such a definition expressed the wish that it be postponed in order to avoid encumbering the Church's doctrine and creating new difficulties in its relations with the Protestants. But since the Pope decided to override these objections, why not present this dogma to the faithful in such a way as to bring home its religious and human significance? Why not comment upon this act of the supreme magisterium in the light of twentieth-century society? Why not point out that the Catholic Church has always had a cult—in the broadest sense of the term

[2] "The dogma of the Trinity," writes Feodorov, "is our social program."

[3] Fr. Marc Oraison, who is both a theologian and psychiatrist, writes: "In a way, one can say that the Christian conception of God—trinitarian mystery and incarnation—is the only one that is really satisfactory to the modern psychologist" (*Devant l'illusion et l'angoisse*, Editions Fayard).

—of woman through Mary? By officially recognizing yet another privilege of the Mother of Christ, the Church places woman at the summit of humanity and of grace;[4] it immediately situates her in the glory of the resurrection of the body which awaits humanity at the end of time.

In this fidelity to the higher law of its faith, the Church is in harmony with the contemporary concern to give woman an increasingly important metaphysical and social status. The twentieth century is gradually becoming the century of the woman (and of the child), on the three levels of thought, culture, and morals.[5] It is also the century of the body and of the rehabilitation of all its functions after the errors of Jansenism and Cartesianism. Both philosophers and scientists are placing more and more emphasis on the value of the body and on its spiritual importance in the complex that is man. The success of

[4] The dogma of the Immaculate Conception had already proclaimed this unique perfection, but where is the average Catholic who knows what the Immaculate Conception is? Who is interested in it? And whose fault is it?

[5] "The modern world," writes Jean Guitton, "is still a masculine world—planned by men and for men, endowed with a masculine culture, with masculine institutions—rather than a properly human world." That is true, but man is in process of losing his supremacy, or, rather, his exclusive status, and, under the gradual influence of Christianity, the day of woman is beginning to dawn. The Church, for its part, by conceding an ever more important place to Mary, is in an era of Marian theology and spirituality. It has thus contributed in no small measure to demasculinizing piety and civilization.

Teilhard de Chardin may perhaps be due in part to this fundamental intuition that matter in general, and the human body in particular, constitutes the matrix of the spirit, and on this account will be "recapitulated" on the day of the Parousia instead of being abandoned like unprofitable servants. Will not the final "Christification" of the world follow a process comparable to that of the historical Incarnation?

In connection with the "fabrication of new species" and with the problem which death poses for modern scientists, M.-A. de Cayeu writes:

> In the beginning there was immortality of the flesh. This idea (very definite and very widespread) never ceases to astonish countless critical minds when Genesis teaches it concerning our first parents. Now science, contemporary biology, declares it to be familiar and places it, like Genesis, at the beginning. There is here an agreement in depth between our science and our faith which is extremely consoling to a Christian. . . .
>
> In the beginning, the beings who peopled the earth, and in whom paleontology sees our first parents, were simple and immortal. Then . . . they became complicated, with two consequences: the temptation to pride, and death; sin and punishment. How all this resembles our doctrine of original sin![6]

[6] *Cahiers d'études biologiques* (Lethielleux).

We might add that it also resembles the doctrine of the resurrection of the body.

Even if these views are not acceptable to all, they are undeniably interesting. And do they not indicate possible new avenues for an intelligent presentation of these two dogmas?

It is often claimed—not without acrimony—that Catholic dogma should be reformulated. Possibly it should, but meanwhile it could very well be presented in more meaningful fashion. Dogmas are instruments for approaching God and achieving a better understanding of the economy of Christianity. They have been defined as "intellectual mediations of an act of communion." Our age is witnessing the rehabilitation of "myths," but psychoanalysis, that new tool whose potentialities have yet to be fully explored, is virtually never used to help people understand the significance and the profundity of religious representations.

Catholicism proposes a vision of the world in its relation to God which the thinkers of our time can perfectly well use. C. G. Jung, for instance, took up these questions in his *Psychology and Religion;* and Charles Baudouin has done likewise in his *Psychanalyse du symbole religieux.* It is probable that the more the psychological sciences advance, the more legitimate in theory and valid in practice the dogmatic representations will appear.

But the dogmatic apparatus of the Church also

needs to be severely simplified. Our era no longer tolerates the chapels, the secret corners in churches, the ornaments, the "devotions," which proliferated in the century of bad taste—the nineteenth—which was not, so far as we know, a century of great faith. The sobriety exemplified in modern art should also characterize religion. Fr. Maydieu was so right in summing up his faith in this single, central, necessary, and sufficient affirmation: "I believe in Jesus Christ, risen from the dead."

Fr. Dubarle, a Dominican and professor of the philosophy of science at the Institut Catholique in Paris, has dealt with these problems with unusual courage:

> We are much more aware, in our day, of the all too human element in religious truth—resulting from a particular form of culture or social life— which remains a part of the traditional baggage of our faith. We are now trying to get rid of it. . . . We are going to realize once more, despite a certain inertia of formulations, the vital richness, the buoyant substance—what one might call the new and evangelical quality—which the faith must have had when it was first formulated. . . .
>
> I realized the extent to which scientific thought had been an instrument of purification for the faith, of deeper penetration of the truth. . . . Our age does not ask us to give up our dogmatic form-

ulations, but to understand their meaning, to understand it with vigorous energy. . . . One condition seems to me to be necessary: that this faith should be radically itself, naked if need be, but with the nakedness of a living body, muscular and strong.

This energetic purification of the faith which Fr. Dubarle calls for should not be confused—and that was the great error of the modernists—with any attenuation of religious truths. There can be no question whatsoever of attacking the historical or "meta-historical" reality of the events of religion; what is needed, on the contrary, is to penetrate this reality more deeply, to open up dimensions which are still concealed. Let there be no mistake about it, what the world needs, and what it expects of the Church, is not a "discounted" faith. If this faith, under the pretext of adaptation, came to regard Christ as no more than a superior type of philanthropist, if the properly supernatural universe of grace were reduced to some form of spiritual naturalism, if religious faith were debased to the level of a belief emptied of its historical and intellectual content, if religion was reduced to a system of morals, Catholicism would become just one more nostrum, having lost both its transcendence and its fecundity. And this would happen just as Protestantism was beginning to emerge victorious from the temptation of liberalism. The

Church may appear, now oversystematic, now too naïve. But it is only by surpassing itself, not by diminishing itself, that it can achieve the renewal, the *aggiornamento,* which Pope John XXIII called for in connection with the Council.

7

A Positive, Historical, Living Religion

Religion is a long reflection on facts
carried by tradition and experienced.
Monsieur Pouget

Progress consists in passing from
words to experience, from fiction to
reality.
Fr. Y. M.-J. Congar

WHEN ARCHBISHOP RONCALLI was papal nuncio in
Paris, he said to a legislator who was a Freemason:
"What keeps us apart? Our ideas? You must admit
that that is not very much!" A jest? Probably—but a
significant one. Later, as Pope John XXIII, he made
the following statement in connection with the Council and the divisions between the Christian Churches
—a statement which the *Osservatore Romano* was at
great pains to interpret: "We shall not seek to deter-

mine who was right and who was wrong. The responsibilities are divided. We shall only say: Let us meet, let us put an end to argument." Some maintain that the Pope went so far as to speak of the "sins of the Church." Visibly distressed by these statements, the semiofficial organ of the Vatican accused the journalists who had reported them of misunderstanding the Pope. Nothing is less certain. On the contrary, there is every indication that the Pope had no objection at all to self-criticism within the Church. Did he not initiate it by inviting the bishops of the whole world to express their grievances and their hopes?[1]

We are daily confronted with the picture of people priding themselves on their ideas, brandishing them like banners, aggressively professing their "faith," as others profess a political ideology, claiming to defend "God's cause alone" (this was for long the subtitle of a militant newspaper), marching forward "armed with quotations," and using them like clubs to strike down their adversaries. And who can tell what vanity, pretentiousness, lack of realism, and

[1] In his book, *Vers le Concile*, published by La Bonne Presse, Georges Huber relates that John XXIII, when he was nuncio in Paris, enjoyed Giovanni Papini's *Letters of Pope Celestine VI to All Mankind*, in which an imaginary pope severely rebukes theologians, monks, the religious, and the laity. When the book appeared, in 1946, it caused an uproar in "right-minded" circles, but Archbishop Roncalli, for his part, declared that, despite some exaggerations, he had found the descriptions contained in the book "humiliating, but not depressing."

perhaps of faith, underly such attitudes? Thus it is that a religious assembly can degenerate into a political rally, with the same slogans, the same rancors, the same relish in crushing the adversary, and, in the end, the same sterility.

In these meetings, these newspapers, these discussions, we are far indeed from the spirit of the Gospel, from the persuasive force of true apostles, from indulgence for others (the obverse of severity toward oneself). How is it that some Catholics regard their religion as an ideology, whereas Christ, in teaching the Good News, presented religious truths that were concrete, alive, laden with history, full of attraction for the pure of heart?

Of course, Christ experienced holy wrath, he uttered maledictions, but he had too great a sense of the human to appeal to men habitually in any other way than by kindness and confidence in their desire to be better.

The true "doctors" of the Church have always placed theology at the service of the spiritual life. In rediscovering the "Fathers of the Church," Christians of the second half of the twentieth century are discovering—better late than never—what religious teaching intended for ordinary people really is.

The intellectual charity of a man like Pope John XXIII—the Pope of ecumenism—and his feeling for others, annoys the traditionalists and all those who pride themselves on looking down upon the "decadent morals" of our time. It is a pity, for the world greatly needs to hear words of concord and of peace, to perceive at last the true face of a Church forgetful of its pride.

"Truth itself is made into an idol," said Pascal. But who quotes Pascal from the pulpit? Who speaks and acts as though he really preferred the Gospel to his own petty constructions, as though he preferred man to ideas?

Distillers of quintessences, arid hearts, minds crammed with rules, what have you done with the spirit? Have you forgotten that the letter kills and that only "deeds instruct"? "Intellectual progress," writes Fr. Congar, "consists largely in passing from words to experience, from phrases learned by rote to conclusions personally experienced, in short, from fiction to reality."

"Necessity and events," we read in Pascal's *Thoughts,* "are the teachers which God himself gives us." They save us from verbal automatism and bloodless principles. As there is a Christian agnosticism, so there is a Christian positivism. The true Christian feeds on facts more than on ideas. And the supreme Christian "fact," after all, is Christ, come to offer his living person in place of principles and moral precepts.

"I am the way, and the truth, and the life." Henceforward, in the economy of the New Testament, the law is Christ. The law is no longer an impersonal code, it is the warmth of a thinking, understanding, and loving being. Christ delivered us from stone idols with sightless eyes and deaf ears. He made us the gift of his person. How much of this essential picture remains in the official catechism? What do we teach our children? What nourishment do we offer them, knowing that it will mark them for life? A set of abstract formulas, a moral code which resembles the Ten Commandments more than the Beatitudes, an intellectual halter with no presence behind it, human or divine.[2]

Question the children who come out of the catechism class. Question them twenty years later; their answers are enlightening. They came in the unconscious hope that they would be taught to live and to love, that they would come to know something of the person of Jesus, of the great prophets, of the history of Israel. Instead, they learned a vocabulary, swallowed a system, droned out the rules of a "closed" moral code. Chiefly, they were bored, and that they will never forget.

Sometimes we catch ourselves dreaming a beautiful dream: the catechism is no longer taught by people who have no idea how to teach! If religious instruction is to be adequate and effective, the first

[2] "We talk too much; we want to say everything, explain everything," writes Fr. Honoré, of the French National Catechetical Center. "We are peddlers of words rather than ministers of the Word. We are not spiritual awakeners, and the children who listen to us are helpless in the face of this verbal flood."

requirement is that the catechist should have received a careful psychological preparation. By what aberration, by what scandalous negligence have we given less care to the training of catechists than to setting up parish movie-projection facilities or athletic fields?

The second requirement is that teachers should know the content of what they are teaching. It is a fact that half the time, even in France, where a renewal is undoubtedly taking place, the catechist fails to get across what should be the essential message of his lessons. Too often his chief aim is still to explain, word for word, the formulas which have to be learned by heart. It is reasonable to sum up the teaching in a set of questions and answers, but on condition not only that both question and answer be simple and clear, but also that, before asking students to commit them to memory, their origin should have been explained.

Before receiving his diploma, a catechist must be fully persuaded of the validity of the following statements:

1. Catholicism is a history, not a system. As such, it is already adapted to children, who, thank God, prefer "stories" to ideas.

2. The Bible—the Old Testament as well as the New, but preferably the latter—should be at the center of all religious instruction. It is not enough to connect doctrine to the Gospel; doctrine must flow

from the Gospel as from its source.[3] Christ's parables are there to be used. The private and public life of Christ is fascinating to children.

3. Judeo-Christianity is the history of a people's relations with God—a people, and not a particular individual. We are only just emerging from the individualist crisis which made of the Christian religion a private affair, whereas it is the point of intersection in the relations between God and man at all times and all places. God, who is himself community (Trinity), made a covenant with a human community. The contact between these two communities constitutes the essence of the Good News. The quarrels, promises, repentance, fidelity, and errors of the Jewish people form the thread of sacred history, the archetype of history as such.

4. The Bible is a love story where, little by little, relations based on law give way to relations based on freedom and intimacy, to a dialogue between persons. It is a love story based on the testimony of sacred writers who tell what they have seen, transmit their own experience. The Bible is concrete from start to finish. It relates facts registered by human eyes, ears, and hands. St. Thomas is in a sense the father of modern science, because he doubted as

---

[3] The best evidence of the lacunae in present-day Catholicism is the urge to add adjectives such as "social" or "evangelical" to the word "Catholicism." Cf. *Pour un catholicisme évangélique,* by René Girault (Editions Ouvrières, 1959).

long as he could not "touch." The Evangelists never depart from everyday life, even when they relate experiences as extraordinary as the Resurrection.

5. The Bible—and the Gospels in particular—is not an account of an uninterrupted succession of miracles or wonders. On the contrary, the philosopher of religion familiar with the environment in which Jesus lived is struck by the paucity of miracles related by the Evangelists.

Nor is sacred history a succession of naïve and childish tales. All religions have their miracles. The originality of Christianity lies elsewhere. In the Genesis story, for instance, it is not the vivid imagery of the seven days, of Adam's rib, of the apple, of the serpent, which matters, but the philosophy of creation which emerges from them—the goodness of the world, the fundamental equality of man and woman, human freedom. We might say the same of all biblical "wonders." They are important for what they signify.

6. Christ transcends the law. For a "closed" morality he substitutes an "open" one. With the Beatitudes, the elementary morality of the Decalogue bursts, so to speak, at the seams. In place of fear, Christ offers trust; for a static sense of duty, interior joy; for documents, the word. The Church has grasped this marvelously in setting tradition above texts, even sacred texts.

7. Spirituality takes precedence over morality.

Union with God, the longing to resemble the be-
loved, come before any self-centered satisfaction in
having observed the rules. In any case, morality is
only a means. "I do not seek virtues," said Teresa of
Avila, "but the Lord of virtues."[4]

An act is not bad because it is forbidden; it is forbidden because it is bad, because it mutilates and
degrades. Virtue is liberation, full-flowering; it abol-
ishes the obstacles to union with God.

8. Sacrifice is never an end in itself; it is a means
of pruning away whatever interferes with the development of the personality; it is a test of love. The
difficulty experienced in performing a good action is
not, as is generally believed, the measure of its moral
value. On the contrary, facility is an indication that
virtue has reached maturity.

9. Christianity trusts man. Christ loves man and
believes in his betterment. Contempt for man is anti-
Christian. The body, matter, are the stepladders of
the soul and spirit. The whole of creation is good because it issued from God; evil, the fruit of a creature's revolt, can, in principle, be overcome. Human
nature has been damaged, but it has also been restored by the sacrifice of the God-Man. Sin itself,
which is an evil, can be used for a greater good. *O
felix culpa!* sings the Church in Holy Week.

There is thus a Christian optimism. There is faith

---

[4] "Morality is a glaze which makes people impervious to grace,"
wrote Charles Péguy.

in the possibility of moral and material progress. Time, duration, afford an opportunity for drawing closer to God. They permit man gradually to redeem and sanctify himself. The ancient circle of fatality is broken. The wheel of time advances, for better or for worse, but not for nothing.

10. Christianity creates joy. "A sad saint is a sorry saint," as the saying goes. Man, created to love and serve God, finds peace only in the accomplishment of God's will, which is not arbitrary, but which coincides with a right conscience and with the deepest exigencies of our being. Grace is not a cloak; it regenerates nature from within. Nature is made for grace. As Louis Lavelle has put it, "Grace, in both senses of the word, is the perfection of nature."[5]

11. Christianity is a simple religion. There is only one commandment, which sums up all the others—to love God and one's neighbor; only one basic dogma from which all the rest derive—the divinity of Jesus; only one basic sacrament—the Eucharist, in which matter worked over by man, namely, bread and wine, is transformed into the body and blood of the God-Man.

12. Christianity is an exacting religion, hostile to any minimum effort. It teaches that one has done nothing until one has tried everything. Its morality and spirituality are the antithesis of the bourgeois ideal which is satisfied with the happy medium.

[5] *Quatre Saints* (Albin Michel).

What Is Catholicism?

Christianity calls for complete generosity, for total giving; it is a *"sportive"* religion, as Brother Roger, Prior of Taizé, so beautifully put it.[6] The Christian is invited to live heroically.

Why not say this to young people, eager for ideals, at the age for self-sacrifice? Christianity is bound to make an impact on youth if it is presented in all its rigor and sobriety. It is because Catholicism has been made into a cut-rate religion that they turn away from it and look elsewhere for some sophisticated reason for living. From juvenile delinquents to beatniks, the problem of youth gone astray is always the same: to beguile the tedium and futility of their mediocre existence by doing something different; to escape the spiritual void; to forget the lack of love which is their lot.

[6] Roger Shutz, *To Live the Life of Today* (Baltimore, Md.: Helicon Press, 1962).

8

Is Catholic Truth "Rightist"?

In order to safeguard life, modernism
sacrificed forms; in order to safeguard forms, traditionalists sacrifice
life.

Cardinal Suhard

ONE HESITATES to speak of two such completely different subjects as religion and politics in the same
breath. It is a fact, however, that the most active
Catholics are believed to be divided into two camps
—the right and the left—or two tendencies—traditionalists and progressives.

This superficial classification would have little importance were it not usually slanderous and a pretext
for deplorable polemics. One has only to read certain religious publications to realize the virulence of
the attacks and their sorry retinue of rash judgments,
insinuations, and calumnies. Catholics of the right

are even more malicious than those of the left: usually it is they who open hostilities. They send reports to Rome, improve on the warnings of the hierarchy, make it a matter of conscience to detect, denounce, castigate the "heretic." In these detractors, the Holy Office finds voluntary—but embarrassing—aides, for since Catholics of the left are reluctant to use the same tactics, an unfortunate one-sidedness is likely to characterize Rome's decisions.

Rightist Catholics seem to occupy a more comfortable position in the Church today than Catholics of the left. For whereas the latter feel entitled to think for themselves, to search for new solutions, to play the prophet, the former are satisfied with reiterating the same pontifical quotations and treading the thousand-times-beaten track. They echo and they flatter. Hence they pass for the most zealous, the most submissive, the most attentive of the faithful, and make their adversaries appear as dangerous revolutionaries, naïve idealists, or even more or less conscious members of a Marxist fifth column. Contemporary examples are too numerous and too fresh in our memories for it to be necessary to go into detail. It is therefore understandable if people outside the Church think that the best Christians are the traditionalists, and that all the others savor more or less of heresy.

Who has not been through it? One has only to endorse the views of theologians concerned to keep the

Church eternally young to provoke an immediate chorus of indignation: "You are not orthodox!" "Have you forgotten Pius IX's *Syllabus*?" "Have you read *Humani Generis*?" "How can you reconcile what you say with this or that pastoral letter?" "With St. Thomas Aquinas?"

From this to claiming that Catholic doctrine is "rightist," that traditionalism is the very root of Catholicism, is only a step—a step quickly taken. A closer look shows that things are fortunately quite different. Catholic tradition, the Church as a whole, as expressed through the voices of its most authoritative "doctors," is neither rightist nor leftist, neither traditionalist nor progressive. The hierarchy has rejected each of these attitudes in turn.

In this context, we are reminded of the masterly letters of the former Archbishop of Paris, Cardinal Suhard, whose theological soundness Pope Pius XII constantly acclaimed.[1]

In his pastoral letter for Lent, 1947,[2] Cardinal Suhard analyzed at length the errors of traditionalism, "which confuses the integrity of doctrine with the preservation of its passing forms," and "identifies

[1] Discouraged by all the attacks which were being made on him by traditionalists, Cardinal Suhard went one day to ask Pius XII's advice. The Pope answered him in substance: "When we were students together at the Gregorian, it was not Fr. Pacelli but Fr. Suhard who won the gold medal as the best theologian. Fear nothing. Carry on, I am with you!"

[2] *Essor ou déclin de l'Eglise* (Editions du Vitrail).

tradition, which is life, with routine, which is death."
He quoted St. Paul urging the Thessalonians (1,
5:19–21): "Do not extinguish the Spirit. . . . But test
all things; hold fast that which is good."

"Does not history show us," wrote Cardinal
Suhard, "that the tactics of enlistment and psychological 'shock' carried out with the support of the
'secular arm' or with propaganda methods of human
fabrication, turn out to be as ineffective as they are
heedless of evangelical freedom?"

On the subject of modernism,[3] Cardinal Suhard
recalled Rome's rejection of a doctrine which led
logically to "depriving the Church of its transcendence," and which confused life with fashion,
and the rights of intelligence with those of sentiment.

"Keep the talent of faith intact and without blem-
ism," prescribed St. Vincent de Lerins. "You have
received gold, give back gold; do not insolently re-
place gold with lead. . . . Say things in a new way,
but without saying new things."

Of course, the preferences of the Roman Church
vary with the different pontificates. There was Pius
IX, and there was Leo XII; there was Pius XII, and
there was John XXIII. The burden of Communism
weighs heavily upon the relations between the

[3] If Cardinal Suhard had written this letter a few years later,
he would probably have substituted "progressivism" for "modernism."

"Christian left" and the hierarchical Church. Rome has difficulty in keeping an even balance between the two camps, and in the meantime the faithful tear each other's eyes out.

But if one takes the trouble to consider the history of the Church as a whole, without arbitrarily isolating a particular century or decade from the rest of tradition, one is forced to recognize that the Church gradually assimilates positions which were at first defended by individuals. In the field of scriptural studies, Catholic exegesis has taken giant steps forward in the past thirty years. As for doctrinal teaching, great changes have taken place. Not twenty years ago, priests were still deriding evolution and scientific determinism from the pulpits. Psychoanalysis was considered a diabolical invention, the refusal to bear arms on grounds of conscience was condemned with horror, sexual perversion aroused only obtuse indignation. The scriptural accounts of creation were taken literally. The polemics over the Dead Sea manuscripts and the Essene prefigurations of Christianity are still fresh in our minds; so are the clashes over the miracles of Lourdes, over visions, stigmata, and prolonged abstinence from nourishment.

On the ecumenical level, who could have hoped, but a short time ago, that theologians would show the understanding for Lutheran or Calvinist positions which they show today? What has become of the old quarrels over the filioque, predestination, the

Real Presence? How many books, formerly on the Index, appear today in the most orthodox libraries simply by reason of the passage of time!

Even the great modernist controversy has been absorbed, forgotten. Not that all its doctrines triumphed—far from it—but, once passions had died down, Catholicism was able to assimilate what was of value in the movement and in some of its desiderata. Men like Renan, Loisy, Couchoud, Bultmann, are at last judged with serenity. Their relative merits are the more readily recognized since the Church refused to compromise on matters of faith. Modernism had trampled on the real content of dogmas, reducing them to useful images. The defense mechanisms of the Church were effective. But substantial gains remain.

No serious theologian today would quarrel with Fr. Rouquette for stating in *Études*: "It is not, a priori, impossible for the Church to restate previous dogmatic formulations in terms of another mentality, with other systems of symbols, for the benefit of another mental age of humanity. Christian faith is not simply an intellectual acceptance of abstract and obscure propositions, but a living adherence of the whole being and of the whole human psyche." Or with this statement by Fr. Liégé: "Let us not be afraid to recognize the relativisms which burden the knowledge which we have through faith—the historical relativism of formulations, the doctrinal relativism of analogical knowledge. *Deus verius cogitatur quam dicitur et verius est quam cogitatur.* This is the whole law of a religion of Incarnation where the transcendent is already possessed in immanence, the eternal in time. For, despite these relativisms, our faith really attains to God."

Not so long ago, such statements would have brought immediate censure upon their authors.

Who, today, would dream of calling Monsieur Pouget's ideas daring? It took the appropriate Roman congregations less than a year to authorize, with only slight changes, the publication of the progressive Colomb catechism, as well as of Feuillet and Robert's *Introduction à la Bible.* These decisions certainly do credit to both censors and consored.

Fr. Teilhard de Chardin was not permitted to publish his works in his lifetime. Today, however, they enjoy such impressive popularity, they are endorsed by such great names, and they have inspired so many conversions, that Rome's suspicions must eventually be allayed.[4]

The French have the deplorable habit of attaching dishonor to works placed on the Index. In fact, a book can be placed on the Index solely for reasons

[4] The works of Teilhard de Chardin are prohibited in seminary libraries and Catholic bookstores in Rome. A curious measure, indeed, which prevents future priests from absorbing ideas regarded as dangerous for them, whereas no restrictions are imposed upon the laity. Are the latter more immune to danger than the former? And, if so, why?

of expediency, because Rome, in its caution, deems the publication of a particular theory dangerous to the faith of simple people for whom it is responsible. The Holy Office has a difficult choice to make between "scandalizing the strong" and "scandalizing the weak." In an article published in November 1958 in *Vérité et Vie*, Mgr. Weber, Bishop of Strasbourg, wrote the following:

It can happen that members of the *avant-garde*, notwithstanding their spirit of discipline, their desire to serve the Church alone, and their prudence, may find themselves curbed, halted, even censured. Why? Because the authorities at a certain echelon judge that their publications, by their content or their wording, might upset or even endanger a part of the clergy or the faithful, might astonish or shock those within the Church who are still, in the words of St. Paul, "little ones" in the faith (1 Corinthians 3:1); they cannot stand such an interpretation, however certain or probable it may be.

Besides the scandal to the weak, there can also be a scandal to the intelligence, and this can occur at all levels. An exegesis closed to the problems raised by biblical scholarship can create uneasiness about the faith in some minds; this will come to a head when the adult is confronted with facts of which he had known nothing. . . . An exegesis that is too closed can also give the impression to more educated people that the Church is afraid of the truth; that it does not dare look things in the face; that it has reservations. The mistaken but practical consequence is a loss of confidence in the Church; we have encountered souls of this kind.

The Church has to have its "officers of orthodoxy." This is a thankless task, but a necessary one in a human society, as are all police forces and militias. It is up to Catholics, by their courage and love of truth, to see to it that this police does not overstep its rights. And it is up to the Council to press vigorously for the necessary reforms of the Holy Office.

In any case, sooner or later the truth carries the day in the Catholic Church. Monsieur Pouget, speaking of the Church, said, "We are the most terrible of democracies, for the truth, even if it is discovered by the lowliest, always triumphs in the end." The Church a democracy? Monsieur Pouget was exaggerating, but it is certain that the Church is not an absolute monarchy, and furthermore that its government is collegial. The dogma of papal infallibility has a restrictive aspect which should not be lost sight of.

No, the spirit of Catholicism is not, whatever some may think, on the side of traditionalism and conservatism. On the contrary—twenty centuries of Church history prove it—it is on the side of progress, movement, youth, the future. Were it not so, Catholicism would have been dead long ago. Countless times the Church has been written off as finished because it tends to react too little and too late. But it always reacts before it is altogether too late.

Christ did not say, "I am a milestone," but "I am the way." Whatever its blunders, the Church always imitates its master in the end. The Church's genius lies in its capacity for assimilation. It finds its medium everywhere, beginning with the pagan culture of antiquity. To realize this, one has to have visited Rome and glimpsed, on the most commonplace stones, the first traces of a Christianity still immersed in Roman civilization. The cause of the Church is the cause of man and of all genuine manifestations of man's thought and vitality. All that is human passes in fact through Christianity.

But the Church, like a living organism, must develop slowly, imperceptibly. Its responsibilities are immense. It is in duty bound to examine with the utmost care any new developments along its path. Its intransigence sometimes seems surprising, for it judges events from a unique standpoint. M. Latreille has put it very well:

The government of the Church has the immense advantage over "secular" governments of being able to envisage problems not so much from a pragmatic point of view, in terms of movements of public opinion, as from the viewpoint of their religious significance; and of being able to take time to commune with God, that is, to reflect, with a very serious awareness of its responsibilities, on the meaning of the facts before it. The result is that, by virtue of a sense of the spiritual that is rarely lacking, and of an unequaled experience of man, the Holy See has clearly discerned the danger of doctrinal error, or the threat to ecclesiastical discipline inherent in a particular practical innovation, however inadequately motivated the judgments of one or another of its tribunals may have been.

Sectarians of the right and of the left, whose religious culture is sometimes so shallow, should try to grasp this if they can: The Church is a mystery, like its founder. It can be judged properly only from within; the very law of love is that it scandalizes those who do not experience it themselves.

The Church is above all leanings. It does not let itself be monopolized by anyone, neither by a theology, however highly recommended, nor, a fortiori, by any political, social, or philosophical clique. The barque of Peter steers its own course, which is not like any other. Many are the false moves and blunders made, as Mgr. Duchesne used to say, but in the end the course proves right, the rudder steady. The Church writes straight with crooked lines. *Etiam peccata* . . .

9

"The Church
Is You!"

The *"consecratio mundi"* is basically
the task of the laity themselves, of
men intimately involved in economic
and social life, who take part in government and in legislative assemblies.
Pius XII

THE CHURCH has often been compared to an army.
Do not both require sacrifice? Do not both show a
taste for order, discipline, pomp, ceremony? Is not
the monk made of the same stuff as the soldier? The
Church has raised patriotism to the rank of a virtue.
Flags float over altars. Has not the claim been made
that to die for one's country is tantamount to baptism
of blood? In its cult of the nation, the Church goes so
far as to bless armies in time of war. And have
not the episcopates on either side of the Rhine
used identical—and therefore contradictory—lan-

guage about the right to take up arms against the foe?

Nevertheless, we must beware of obvious parallels. The Church is not an army, even though it is called "militant." The tendency to confuse sword and holy-water sprinkler is only too prevalent. The Church is not a barracks, nor the layman an enlisted man. The bishop is not a colonel, nor the Pope some all-powerful general whose ukases cause heads to bow and minds to capitulate. The teaching Church (the bishops gathered around the Sovereign Pontiff) does not have absolute power over the learning Church (priests and laity). The teaching Church is also taught—if only by the Holy Spirit! And the learning Church also teaches: the priest from his pulpit, parents when they give their children religious instruction. We must be careful, therefore, not to overwork these convenient but equivocal expressions.

The word "Church" most often signifies the hierarchy or clergy. How many "good" Catholics say "they" when they mean their Church—like a disgruntled citizen referring to the government—as though the laity were merely passive members of the Church! This attitude is a consequence of the "fighting theology" elaborated to combat the excesses of the Reformation, and the damage it has done the Church itself is incalculable.

Cardinal Gasquet once told this anecdote: A catechumen asked a priest what was the position of the layman in his Church. "It is twofold," the priest replied. "The layman kneels before the altar—that is his first position; he sits facing the pulpit—that is his second position." Cardinal Gasquet added: "There is a third position which the priest forgot to mention —the layman reaches for his wallet."[1]

This mentality is still prevalent. It suffices to attend Mass at any chance stopover to realize how passive the faithful are.

This brings a personal reminiscence to mind. During their captivity between 1940 and 1945, some young French officers had asked a Dominican to lecture to them about the Church, and the priest had entitled his talk, "The Church Is You!" An obviously "right-minded" colonel heard of this title and expressed his disapproval. "These young lieutenants are the Church! Whatever next! What demagogues those Dominicans are!"

The Dominican was right, however, and there was nothing of a demagogue about him. He was simply forthright, and he sensed what these young men, with their middle-class background and far from adequate religious education, needed to be told.

For some years now, the laity have been told repeatedly that they are the Church, though they have not as yet been able to work out all the implications

[1] Related by Fr. Y. M.-J. Congar in *Jalons pour une théologie du laïcat* (Editions du Cerf), a work which the Council is making increasingly pertinent.

of this doctrine. Of course, in a sense the laity will always be a subordinate category, but they are, nonetheless, organically speaking, full members of the Church, with all the rights and responsibilities such membership entails. They are now assuming the functions in the Church which are properly theirs: Catholic Action is their province; they are taking over jobs which priests held only because there was no one else to fill them. The theology of the laity will be clarified by the Council. The new Canon Law, which is already being elaborated, will give the laity official standing.

The "awakening" of the laity is one of the most remarkable phenomena of the twentieth-century Church. The change which is taking place in the Church, and which is really only a return to the sources, has been brought about not only by the shortage of priests, but also by the progressive secularization of society. One of the signs of the growing importance of the laity in the Church is the recent proliferation of "secular institutes"—groups of Christians who remain in the world, in their families if they wish, and in their jobs, but who belong to religious societies aimed at the evangelical perfection of their members. For centuries, monks were laymen, and it is a mistake to identify the "religious" state with the sacerdotal function. Laymen used to be appointed cardinals. Francis of Assisi was not a priest, neither were the first Franciscans. Neither was Charles de Foucauld at the outset of his religious life.

Theologians speak of the "priesthood of the faithful" conferred by the sacraments of baptism and confirmation. The laity are explicitly called upon to take part in the hierarchical apostolate. Their mission is to "consecrate the world," this world in which they live and which they alone know well, not being separated from it like the priest by a special mode of life. Cardinal Suhard could envisage priests becoming workers[2] only as an attempt to close the rift between workers and the Church, but this exceptional form of apostolate was created to answer an exceptional need. Workers' Catholic Action groups finally realized this, having balked at first at what they felt might be a new form of clericalism.

The priest is at the service of the laity. It is among them that he carries on his activities. Who, if not the layman, can tell him whether his words have been heard and understood, whether they have struck home? Who, if not the layman, will tell the priest about the attitude of his parishioners, their needs, expectations, difficulties? How can a parish be a living community if the laity keep their problems to

[2] Jean Guitton discerns in the idea of the worker-priest "a new conception of the incarnation of the consecrated man amongst men." "The worker-priest," he writes, "reminds us of the man of sorrows spoken of by Isaia, without beauty in him, nor comeliness, as a root out of a thirsty ground" (Isaia 53:2). (From his *Journal*, Plon, 1959.)

themselves, if they do not take the clergy to task where necessary, or encourage them as they deserve? "The laity," Canon Law prescribes, "have the right to receive from the clergy, according to the rules of ecclesiastical discipline, spiritual benefits and the helps necessary for their salvation" (Canon 682). It is up to the laity, then, to demand much of their priests, to complain of their inadequacies, to praise their achievements. A two-way relationship should exist between them, as in a family where each member, according to his function, contributes to the common good. What can be more discouraging for a priest than to feel himself isolated, criticized behind his back, or treated with contempt? In the ecclesial community, authority comes from above, but vitality comes from all sides. It behooves the humblest of the laity as well as the most outstanding of the clergy to propose the reforms which the Spirit prompts them to propose.

José de Broucker told the following story upon his return from Indo-China: When a priest of the Christian community of Viet Nam is inadequate, the laity send a delegation to the bishop to inform him of the fact. If no action is taken, they take the priest, set him on a sedan chair, and carry him to the bishop, saying, "Keep him, we don't want him any more; give us another priest." Such methods, of course, are not for export, but they are evidence of a vital community.

What Is Catholicism?

Bishops, in former times, were elected directly by the people. Even if this custom cannot be restored, it would be desirable that the bishop be chosen from among names proposed by qualified representatives of a diocese. The present system of nominations has aroused justifiable criticism.

The centralization of the Church, as at present constituted, leaves an insufficient margin of freedom and autonomy to bishops and laity. The Council will have to undertake reforms in this area. Some system must also be found to enable national Churches to discuss matters with the Vatican and to defend their points of view. The best remedy for certain rather clumsy interventions by Rome would be to set up more logical internal structures, and at the same time to choose men of strong character as bishops. The danger of Gallicanism is far enough behind us to rule out any serious objections to such reforms. At the present time, the French laity are not sufficiently organized in relation to their clergy and episcopate, nor the episcopate in relation to Rome. Alternatives must be found to ensure a better balance and a distribution of authority more in harmony with the evolution of society and the complexity of its problems.

The Church will reach the world—which in some ways is growing increasingly estranged from the Church—to the extent that it learns to trust the rank and file, and revises certain methods of command conceived in an outmoded framework of Christendom.

As for the laity, if some among the best of them aspire to play a more effective part within their Church, they must make a great effort to overcome their individualism and their propensity for criticism. Criticism is not an evil if it constitutes a basis for action. But what usually happens? Everything that goes wrong in a parish is blamed on someone else. People are content to complain about the pastor or the bishop—they lament about all the red tape. What point is there in all this unless a man is determined to take some personal action in the matter?

Middle-class communities are especially spineless. Egotism is the permanent temptation of the comfortably-off. To the extent that parishioners belong to the social upper stratum, they seem to be less interested in the life of their parish. The more they have received from society, the less disposed they seem to devote themselves to it. At the same time, the least generous are the most demanding. It is the fashion, in some circles, to deplore priests' lack of culture or distinction. But if a young man thinks of entering the priesthood, his parents immediately protest and do everything they can to make him change his mind. "My son is much too sensitive, much too intelligent to be a priest!" That is the world's logic.

Whenever Christians criticize their parish, one is entitled to ask them: "What are you doing to im-

prove it?" In religion, as in politics, those who do
not personally try to remedy the evils they denounce
forfeit the right to complain.

There are not two Churches, that of the priests
and that of the laity. "The Church cannot cloister itself, inert, in the recesses of its temples," said Pius
XII, "and forsake the mission entrusted to it to fashion the whole man, and thereby to collaborate in
establishing a sound foundation for society. This
mission is essential to the Church. . . . From this
point of view, the laity are in the front ranks of the
Church's life; through them, the Church is the vital
principle of society. . . . They are the Church."

The Church is made up of all the baptized, of all
ranks and all ages. It is the community of all the
faithful, the just and the sinners, on pilgrimage together toward the kingdom of God, of which this
earth, redeemed by Christ, has already received the
pledge.

The invisible Church is the flood tide of all men of
good will, whatever creed they may profess—or of no
creed at all—as long as they try to follow the voice
of conscience. It is, above all, the wretched, the hungry, the despised. It is also the rich whose souls are
pure enough not to be consumed with greed and selfishness. The Church is the mystical body of Christ;
it is Jesus Christ continued in time and space; it is
the immense flock of men of every race and every
color who possess a sense of justice and of truth; it is

the peaceful army of men who believe in men, who do not ridicule progress, who are determined to rebuild with generosity what selfishness and cowardice are constantly destroying. Beyond the frontiers of the visible Church, recognizable by the seal of the sacraments, lies the invisible Church, gathering up the living forces of mankind, as they painfully give birth to a more fraternal world. It is not secularizing the Church unduly to acknowledge its presence wherever a spark of charity glows or a stalk of flax still smolders. "Not everyone who says to me, 'Lord, Lord,' shall enter the kingdom of heaven; but he who does the will of my Father . . ." (Matthew 7:21)

The visible Church, the Church "militant," veritable bridgehead of mankind, is the perceptible nucleus of those who live in contact with the sacraments, the normal channels of grace. The mission of this society, embodied in institutions organically linked with the first Christians, is to draw all creation to itself and to go out to look for the sheep which do not yet know it.

The Church is missionary or it is nothing. If it shuts itself in on itself, and becomes a ghetto, it betrays itself. The Church should never tire of calling with compassion to those outside. As the custodian of the Gospel leaven, it has the duty to teach all nations. But the property of leaven is its power to make dough rise. The Church is recognizable by the fact that it does not hide its light. Universal by right, it must slowly, with living stones, build up the community of man, build up the body of Christ together with all creation, "restore all things in Christ," as St. Paul put it.

10
The Church, a
"Machine for Making Gods"

> Christianity gives man his full stature,
> and more than his stature. It calls
> upon him to be a god, and it calls
> upon him in freedom; that, for the
> Christian, is the ultimate and supreme
> significance of historical develop-
> ment.
>
> Emmanuel Mounier

It has to be said, because it is the truth—a blinding
truth in this century of Nazi crematories and charnel
houses, of Soviet trials, of mass deportations and
events such as the Hungarian tragedy: The disciples
of Nietzsche and Goering, of Marx and Stalin, all
who have sought to kill God and put man in his
place, have ended up debasing man's soul and despising his body. The Inquisition, with its burnings
at the stake; the Middle Ages, that alleged golden

age of Christianity; the massacre of St. Bartholomew and others like it during the wars of religion—all these pale in comparison with modern horrors. Moreover, there is a notable difference. Christians do not try to justify these perversions; they are ashamed of them and ask God's pardon.

It has to be said, because it is the truth: Those who accuse Christianity—not without some justification—of being the opium of the people, those who want to deliver man from the "yoke" of his Creator and Redeemer, have bartered real spiritual deficiencies and a social conservatism marked by selfishness for a disastrous spiritual void and an incitement to hatred whose fruits are hardly attractive.

And it also has to be said, because it is the truth: Christianity is the first Western religion to set itself the task of "divinizing" man. "You are gods," St. Paul told the members of the early Church. And each day, at Mass, the priest recalls that the Christian "shares the divinity" of Jesus *(ejus divinitatis esse consortes)*.[1] "God became man," wrote two doctors of the Church, "so that man might become a god."

The atheist philosophers of the nineteenth century who made a god of man did no more than adapt a distorted form of the Christian "myth." Christianity gave Western man the idea, then the desire, to become a god. Without Christianity, Nietzsche would

---

[1] See also 2 Peter 1:4: "so that . . . you may become partakers of the divine nature. . . ."

probably never have invented his "superman." Nor would Marx have made history his god, for evolution, faith in man and in progress, are ideas of Christian origin, false in what they deny, not in what they affirm.

It is absurd to claim that Nietzsche and Marx can be explained by their pride alone. The greatness of these atheists lies precisely in their rejection of a caricature of God which alienates man, and of a Church which preaches only resignation. They are right in denying such counterfeits.[2] Their mistake lies in their inability to discover the living God behind these lies, and the true Church behind its false façade.

Christians will not achieve anything just and effective simply by rejecting the aspirations of these philosophers, but only by assuming and transcending them. "The more man is man," wrote Fr. Chenu, "the more chance God has of being God."

We cannot be content simply to oppose Nietzsche's superman and Marx's earthly paradise with the concept of Christian humility or of this world as a "vale of tears." They must be countered with the pride and creative will of man grafted in God and regenerated by grace.

The Christian's vocation is to draw ever closer to

2 Jean Lacroix writes in *Le sens de l'athéisme moderne*: "Marx's atheism is the necessary corollary of his positive definition of man as essentially a worker, who achieves his humanity by transforming the world. . . . Camus asks: 'What generates charity if not atheism?' "

his divine model until, after the final metamorphosis, he enjoys the very life of his Creator. The beatific vision, which the ignorant deride, is an apotheosis, not a resignation, and it has to be prepared for on this earth. Blame for the bondage of thought or human laziness should not be placed on the Gospel but on the caricatures fashioned by those who have betrayed the Christian ideal, even if they were authorized to propagate it.

After years of sectarian materialism, it was Bergson, finally, who made our contemporaries realize once more that the saint and the mystic are greater and more effective than the hero or the political demiurge; who rediscovered that "the universe is a machine for making gods," and that Jesus is the incomparable prototype of humanity. Where, except in Christianity, should one find that "extra soul-life" which Bergson called for in the modern world? Where, but in the evangelical ideal and among those who live it, should we look for the joy of life which is so lacking in a generation made captive by material progress? One has only to see its flowering in the contemplative orders.

The vitality of the Russian Church, the fervor of its faithful, are proof that man, even Soviet man, does not live by bread alone.

If the universe is a "machine for making gods," the Church is the soul and nucleus of this expanding universe, the mistress of joy and hope, the tireless teacher. It alone has received the promise of permanence which will enable it, to the end of time, directly to promote the spiritual advancement of the children of God and, indirectly, their material advancement.

Again it must be said, because it is true, and because it tends to be forgotten, that Christianity has identified love of God with love of neighbor. "If anyone says, 'I love God,' and hates his brother, he is a liar" (1 John 4:20).[3] The man who truly loves his neighbor and serves him, even if he does not believe in God, is closer to God than the man who says he loves God and lives in selfishness, pride, laziness, and passivity. It is in this sense that Christianity assimilates unbelief. We have all known people of outstanding merit who have left the Church because they were disillusioned with what they saw of it, yet who constantly practice true Christian charity. To these, on the last day, Christ will say, as he himself announced, "As long as you did it for one of these, the least of my brethren, you did it for me. . . . Come, blessed of my Father . . ." (Matthew 25:40, 34). We shall be judged by love.

The God of Christians does not release man from all effort and initiative. On the contrary, he asks us

---

[3] According to Berdyaev, no philosophical or even theological research can begin with the study of either God or man; it must begin with the theandric nature which governs this opposition. "In Christ," he wrote, "man sees the face of God, and in turn knows his own."

to make every effort to transform the world, starting with ourselves. The true Christian acts as though everything depended on him alone. "I treat, and God cures," is the cry of faith. The "duty of one's state in life," as catechetical jargon has it, comes before religious observance. A good priest does not go off to recite his breviary if his brother calls him urgently. The Levite who passed the wounded man on the road to Jericho was perhaps on his way to a religious service. And Christ reproved him for not helping his brother.

To work with a pure heart is to pray, even if one believes that heaven is empty, for it is collaboration in the work of creation. It is futile to oppose action and contemplation. The "theology of work" dear to Fr. Chenu[4] is still pending. And unfortunately it needed the Communist thrust to awaken Christians to the sacred character of work.

God gave the world over to man to organize and administer. Man is the world's priest in the footsteps of Christ; his work "divinizes" him, and at the same time the universe. This means that to create, whether with hands or brain, is to advance the kingdom of God, hastening the hour when the world will be mysteriously transfigured by the Spirit.

God became man, and then, more mysteriously still, bound his presence to the consecration of bread and wine, those fruits of man's labor. In the Mass,

[4] See M. D. Chenu, *La théologie du travail* (Editions du Cerf).

Christ offers the creative effort of men to the Father through the priest.

Why, then, do so many Christians go along with dull eye and dangling arms, resigned to some kind of destiny, abandoning to unbelievers the task of bringing creation to completion? If the salt loses its strength, what shall it be seasoned with?

Why, if not because religious ignorance is the thing most evenly distributed? Because those who profess to teach Christianity no longer know how to translate the Gospel. Because they parrot Revelation in the language of textbooks dating from the Renaissance. Because they forget their gripping vocation as mediators and interpreters. Experience proves that where bishop and clergy know how to speak to contemporary man, churches are filled, parishes revive, the poor have the Gospel preached to them, workers swallow their anticlericalism.

How should it be otherwise when men are shown that already in this world they are called to become gods, by their daily work, and by the offering of their efforts to him who accepted the cross to save them?

11
Miracles
in Abeyance?

> Catholic miracles make the ignorant
> laugh, but a minimum of culture
> makes it plain, on the contrary, that
> Catholicism must be considered as
> the first religion without miracles; not
> absolutely without miracles, but al-
> ways reasonable and wary about
> them. . . .
>
> Alain

"TAKE THE MIRACLES out of the Gospel and all the
earth will be at the feet of Jesus Christ!" This sally
of Jean-Jacques Rousseau's still finds an echo in our
day. Our contemporaries are afraid of being taken
in by extraordinary phenomena. The fact that science cannot explain them is no longer a sufficient
reason for men to be willing to attribute such phenomena to the direct action of God. Should a religious person deplore this skepticism, or should he

rather welcome it as a sign of progress? The field of miracles seems to shrink in proportion as science and psychology extend their investigations. Will the day come when miracles, as conceived so far, will disappear altogether? Or will they remain as the "thorn of irrationality"[1] which cannot be removed?

Miracles, traditional apologetics teaches, attest to the existence of God and his action in the world. They are the most outstanding sign of divine omnipotence. They should, it is sometimes added, confound the unbeliever who is in good faith. In practice, priests use this argument less and less. Rather than a help to faith, miracles constitute an additional obstacle. For the handful of individuals whose unbelief miracles have shaken, there are scores who react in just the opposite way: for the most part, the believer believes in spite of miracles.

We will not discuss the miracles of the Gospel here. One reason is that they are too distant for an unbeliever seriously to set about verifying their authenticity. How can it be proved to him, for example, that Lazarus came back to life? Has such a wonder been seen since? Furthermore, for the believer, the Gospel is part of Revelation—which is closed with the last line of the Bible—and in principle, nothing is opposed to the Son of God having received extraordinary powers.[2]

---

[1] The expression is Maurice Blondel's.
[2] Christ's resurrection is, properly speaking, a mystery rather than a miracle.

On the other hand, contemporary miracles constitute a firm basis for discussion. The Church, in its wisdom, has taken great care not to make them an article of faith. When an apologist ventures to write: "The miracle of Lourdes imposes belief in the supernatural"—he was writing, it is true, in 1913—he speaks only for himself, and no longer persuades anyone. This position, furthermore, is suspect to orthodoxy, which teaches that faith is a free act. No fact, then, can impose it. Grace is always necessary for a miracle to seem conclusive, and it is with the greatest prudence that we must interpret the definition of the Vatican Council: "A miracle is a sign that is very sure and is adapted to the intelligence of all."

Why do miracles present a difficulty? Essentially, it seems, for two reasons.

First of all, we live in a scientific age which has eliminated God as the explanation of natural phenomena. Our ancestors attributed to God whatever they did not understand—lightning, thunder, the rainbow, sudden cures. Kings who cured scrofula seemed invested with divine power. If not God, then the devil was held responsible. Today we know better. Science has shown us new mechanisms of nature, as well as the unexpected effects of depth psychology. Levitation, clairvoyance, telepathy, are far from perfectly understood, but those who are studying them take them seriously, precisely because they think they can be explained.

Secondly, the scientist, by definition, ignores the

supernatural; it is the very condition of scientific progress. "Science," Fr. Bouillard rightly points out, "cannot even conceive of the notion of miracles." In this respect, it has done an immense service to religion; it has helped strip it of a thousand naïvetés which were damaging its prestige. The Catholic Church has shown great perspicacity in carefully screening popular beliefs. Its attitude to Lourdes is characteristic. It accepted Bernadette's story only after much hesitation. And when it finally capitulated before the good sense and exceptional persistence of this child, it did not thereby ratify all the wonders of which Lourdes has been the scene. On the contrary, it has succeeded in making of this place of pilgrimage, on the one hand, a place of prayer, and on the other, a place of medical reflection. Everyone knows how responsibly the members of the bureau for the ascertainment of the medical facts now operate. The conditions which must be met before a cure can be certified are extremely severe. So much so that the number of miracles recognized by the Church following the doctors' screening has constantly diminished, while the number of the sick registered at Lourdes has increased. Here are some figures: From 1894 to 1908—100 to 235 cures annually; from 1926 to 1938—ten; from 1939 to 1950— fifteen *in all*. In 1930, one miracle was recognized for five thousand pilgrims; in 1949, one for one million. As the progress of medicine leads doctors to be increasingly circumspect before certifying a case, we can foresee that the number of official miracles will move toward zero.

Dr. Pierre Mauriac, a Catholic, did not hesitate to state before the Marian Congress at Lourdes: "Time will not spare medical opinions on the cures at Lourdes. The way things are going, barely ten years from now, observations which in 1958 seem to us hardly disputable will be as discredited as those of fifty years ago."

But for the moment, the fact remains. Cures are registered at Lourdes which are "inexplicable in the present state of science." Whether there are few or many does not change the problem. A single miracle would suffice to call everything into question again.

Paul Valéry said ironically: "God's contempt for human minds is evident in miracles. He judges them unworthy of being moved toward him by other paths than those of stupefaction and the coarsest modes of sensitivity." The objection is not easy to refute if the miracle is considered only in its outward manifestation. Christ himself reproached his contemporaries: "Unless you see signs and wonders, you do not believe" (John 4:48). It even happened that he refused to work miracles because of the hardness of men's hearts.[3] However, if we consider the inner significance of the miracle, it appears, on the contrary, as a sign of the goodness of God, who takes

[3] Mark 8:11.

pity on suffering and puts an end to it by appropriate means. "Ask and you shall receive," he said. At Lourdes, precisely, the pilgrims call upon the divine mercy.

But, it may be objected, how is it, then, that there are so few cures, and that these seem to be distributed at random? Is it not more satisfying to the mind to suppose that the rare cures on record are the fruit of natural mechanisms which are not yet understood? All the more so since the dead have never been known to rise at Lourdes, nor limbs to grow back, nor has any other phenomenon taken place which is directly contrary to the laws of nature.

Professor Jean Lhermitte, another Catholic doctor, commenting on the cure of P. de Rudder, one of the most famous at Lourdes, writes: "The restoration of the bone is very defective; there is an angulation of the tibia and fibula which would have been very severely judged had it been effected by an orthopedic surgeon." In the Cahiers Laënnec, Dr. Lafitte states, concerning the same case: "Everything took place as though a good practioner, concerned to restore the solidity and the direction of the leg's axis without shortening it . . . had reduced and set the fracture, which subsequently mended. But all this work, which usually requires several weeks, even several months, took place *instantaneously*. Therein lies the phenomenon which upsets all accepted notions of bone pathology. Therein is the sign of an intervention which

166

we cannot know or control. Therein is the miracle."

It seems, indeed, that the rapidity, or the quasi-instantaneous nature of the cure, is today the only incontestable criterion of the miracle. It all happened, says Dr. Mauriac further, as though "a heavy foot pressed down the accelerator and all the speed records were broken. God shows that he can get a performance from the machine he has created which no medical force has yet been able to achieve. Why God?" he goes on to ask; "physiology contains so many unknown forces that the difficulties which stop us today will be child's play for the next generation. Not to speak of the parapsychic potential, which has hardly been tapped; not to speak of the soul, which perhaps does not play a passive role."

Here we touch the heart of the problem. All that nature teaches us leads us to believe that, even in miracles, God acts, as usual, through the agency of secondary causes. Can we have reached, in this second half of the twentieth century, the last era when it can still reasonably be believed that God intervenes directly through miracles?[4] Is this perhaps childish approach not becoming progressively un-

[4] "A purification is necessary," writes Fr. Chenu, "as a result of which, what is really sacred, including what is sacred in biblical history, will not be obscured by the transition to the profane implicit in the autonomy of human action. Recognition of secondary causes does not mean setting the first cause aside, but, on the contrary, glorifying it precisely where its generosity is most conspicuous."

tenable? In asking a tribunal of doctors to examine the cures of Lourdes, so that only the really inexplicable cases are certified, is not the Church walking into a trap? We have already pointed out that the number of recognized miracles is constantly decreasing. If the Lourdes medical bureau does not change its methods, are we not likely to see, in the not so distant future, the death of miracles? In any case, it will be to the Church's honor that it placed itself voluntarily on its adversaries' ground, putting God to the test, so to speak, to see whether he was really the author of the cure. Even if this method ends in a stalemate, the Church will emerge the greater for it. If scientific criticism kills the traditional concept of the miracle, it will be a victory for truth, in which Christians can only rejoice. This is the way the faith is purified of its prejudices, and remains eternally young.

For the essential thing about a miracle, in the eyes of the Church, is not its prodigiousness, but the fact that a phenomenon particularly striking to the imagination is interpreted as a "sign" from God. It matters little, basically, whether science succeeds or not in explaining the process of a cure. What is important in the last analysis is the purity of the context in which the phenomenon takes place. The Church does not decide that a miracle has taken place solely because the cure is reputed to be inexplicable, but chiefly because this cure took place in an atmosphere of faith and because those who witnessed it discern in it an answer. "Being inexplicable does not make a thing supernatural," writes Dr. Mauriac, "for if this were so, doctors would be miracle workers and the hospital a court of miracles. . . . The inexplicable does not in itself imply the miraculous."

The special intervention of God in nature and in the complex of secondary causes was alien to St. Augustine's vision. For this Church Father, remarks Fr. Liégé, creation is in a habitual state of obedience to God, and essentially supple. If miracles are unusual, they are so only in contrast with phenomena to which we are accustomed and concerning which our attention has been dulled. But is it not just as marvelous, in itself, that God makes the grape swell on the vine or the grain of wheat germinate? Everything is a sign of God for the religious soul.

From this point of view, the miracle would be a special sign only because of its strangeness, and not because science cannot account for it. The truly great, permanent miracle is the whole of creation, which science will probably never explain. The inexplicable is not on the level of secondary causes, but on that of the first cause, which is extrascientific by definition.

If this hypothesis were to be verified in the years to come, the notion of miracles would be modified, but would remain intact. The task of the Lourdes medical bureau would be simplified. It would not have to eliminate all cures which could probably be explained by science, but only the frauds, or those which have no objective interest. Fundamentally, after a long purification in response to rationalist exigencies, it would mean the rediscovery of a more interior conception of miracles.[5] A miracle would then be held to be everything which seemed an answer to a prayer.

Hope and faith can be factors in healing. "Faith healing," before it was a theory, was an observed fact. By what mechanism? The answer is up to the scientists. Christ put it strongly enough: "If you have faith like a mustard seed, you will say to this mountain, 'Remove from here'; and it will remove" (Matthew 18:19).

It would be illogical if the virtue of faith, the first of the theological virtues and the fruit of grace, were to have no effect on matter. Healers who do no more than make use of their patients' confidence in their own human power sometimes obtain undeniable results. How much more so should faith in God. Trustful prayer is in itself a factor making for psychic balance. Why should not the psychic mechanism

[5] "The supernatural, the miracle, can always appear on second reading, and like a watermark, in nature itself. The supernatural is not the negation of nature but its final and most secret meaning for the faithful conscience," wrote Georges Gusdorf, a Protestant professor of philosophy at the University of Fribourg, in a pamphlet on the relation of science and faith published by the *Revue de l'Evangélisation*, No. 65, at 47 rue de Clichy, Paris IX.

which serves as a relay between the spiritual and the material universe also serve as an intermediary between nature and grace?

If this viewpoint were confirmed, the miracle would no longer appear as an exceptional phenomenon. On the contrary, it would be seen as obeying an inner logic, still mysterious, and perhaps to remain so for a long time to come, but it would no longer be an effect without a natural cause. Miracles are not magic; they are unusual phenomena produced by unusual causes.

Are miracles in abeyance? Perhaps, if we insist on considering them as an irrational wonder. Surely not, if we consent to see them as natural phenomena which a believer links with the providential action of God in the world. A miracle is a special case where "the mark of God" appears more obviously than in the usual phenomena of nature. The difference is one of degree, really, not of kind. It is for the scientists, in the first place, and then for the philosophers and theologians, to decide whether this interpretation, which conforms to the Augustinian vision, is more accurate than the interpretation which has been current since the time of St. Thomas Aquinas.

12
Secularism, a Christian Invention

> The process of secularization, however perverted and clumsy in its operation, is not only a fact of history, but it also gives effect, in great travail, to the evangelical principle of the transcendence of the Word of God.
>
> Fr. Chenu

> Every paganism is a form of clericalism, and the converse, basically, also holds.
>
> Joseph Vialatoux

How CAN secularism be in conformity with Christian doctrine? To most of those concerned, it is not very apparent. The ideals of liberty, equality, and fraternity might perhaps be recognized as offshoots of

Christian principles, but what a paradox to maintain that secularism is the fruit of nineteen centuries of Christianity!

Suppose we look at the lesson of history—the history of facts and ideas. Does it not teach that it is in the nature of Christianity to "desacralize the world," as Jean Lacroix puts it?

Before Christ, throne and altar literally merged into one. The pagan civilizations spontaneously vested religious and political authority in a single leader. To disobey man was thus to disobey God. The tyrant's caprice had the force of civil and religious law.

The teaching of Jesus, the greatest revolutionary of all times, upset these sacrosanct principles.[1] Christ came to teach men—who are still amazed and even scandalized about it—that his kingdom was not of this world; that it was better to obey God than men. The famous injunction: "Render . . . to Caesar the things that are Caesar's, and to God the things that are God's" (Matthew 22:21), dropped casually from Jesus' lips, tolled the knell of a certain type of civilization. For nineteen centuries, it is true, the knell has not stopped tolling. Periodically, modern tyrants, in their pride, refuse to hear it and set about relentlessly "sacralizing" their authority. They exhort the human flock to "absolutize" and to "deify," if not

[1] Mgr. Marty, Archbishop of Rheims, wrote: "The Holy Spirit is both a disturber and a constructor."

173

their person, at least a particular principle—whether race, or nation, or—most subtle of poisons—history. When an encyclical condemns Fascism, Nazism, *atheist* Communism, it is only repeating, in modern terms, the fundamental principle of Catholicism, namely, that God alone is absolute, and that everything else, however great it may be, is relative. The spheres of the sacred and the profane are distinct. To set up the profane as sacred is indeed the mark of paganism.[2]

The history of the world is the history of a growing awareness—with its high and low points—of the distinctions to be drawn between the sacred and the profane, the relative and the absolute. The greater the advance of civilization, the further the notion of the sacred recedes, while the secular world gains in scope, coherence, and autonomy.

The history of the Church itself, so closely bound up with secular history, reflects this tendency. The process sometimes appears exasperatingly slow, but it goes forward nonetheless. And the advance of religious or civil societies hangs by this golden thread. In some ways, the Middle Ages and the Renaissance were still caught in the toils of paganism. Providence perhaps used the temporal power of the Popes

2 "The idea of a secular state," wrote Joseph Vialatoux, "could have arisen only in a personalist civilization leavened by Christianity. The secular state can germinate only in Christian soil. . . . It is the state realizing the spiritual limits of its sovereignty and observing those limits."

and the higher clergy to advance the cause of religion, but in the manner that evil is used to bring about a greater good. Clericalism is the worst internal enemy of the Church. It is based on the confusion of two distinct spheres. Cardinal Gerlier recently stated it thus: "Clericalism, which is the tendency of a spiritual society to meddle in the political sphere of the state, is contrary to the authentic thinking of the Church."[3]

The Church, of course, has often succumbed to this temptation. But those who criticize churchmen for taking advantage of circumstances to interfere in the political sphere should remember that their own exacting demands are the fruit of a Christian education, whether they realize it or not. It is in the name of Christianity itself that clericalism is to be condemned.

Two thousand years of Christianity have enriched the content of natural morality, the morality, that is, which does not take its stand explicitly on God, but on conscience. For better or for worse, the Churches have played the part of educators of the human race.

[3] Speech to the legislators assembled at Lourdes in August 1958.
"The clericalism of inadequate Christians," wrote Joseph Vialatoux, "corrupts the secularism of the state by inciting the state to shut itself up in a supposed anticlericalism which in truth is only clericalism back to front, a clericalism of irreligion; this, in turn, strengthens the supposed religious clericalism which it opposes. This vicious circle, of which our history furnishes lengthy examples, is largely responsible for our difficult politico-religious problems."

Under their influence, the general moral sense has been sharpened. Only the blind would deny it. Thus modern man, generally speaking, has an increased awareness of the solidarity of all men, a jealous love of freedom, an extraordinary sensitivity with regard to social justice, and a respect for the life and dignity of other men unparalleled in any previous age. Would the motto of the French Revolution have been conceivable in any unevangelized country?

This progress of the moral conscience, which no longer relies on a religion, or even on theism, has led to various declarations of human rights—that of 1791 in France, for instance, and that proclaimed in 1948 by the United Nations, where the emphasis is on the economic and social aspirations of communities. Of the latter, Fr. Chenu wrote that it constituted "an impressive advance" in the moral history of peoples. Jacques Maritain, who was at the time French Ambassador to the Holy See and chairman of the French delegation to the UNESCO conference, referred in this connection to "the possible foundations of a common human *credo*" for all civilized nations—the expression was Teilhard de Chardin's. M. Maritain expressed satisfaction that humanity should be gradually reaching agreement on broad principles beyond all religious sanction, and spoke of "the vegetative growth of moral perception," an extension of what the theologians call the "natural law."

Political and religious tolerance is a modern acquisition, a victory over sectarianism and fanaticism. "I would mistrust a religion which claimed to have a 'corner' on truth," said Gabriel Marcel. And it would be disastrous if Catholics gave the impression that they "possessed" the truth, whereas they do no more than receive it, and whereas this truth has for them a name and a face—Jesus. What could be more scandalous than wars of religion between Christians redeemed by the same blood!

Secular morality, as long as it does not try to tie itself implicitly to a definite philosophical system (which is unfortunately not always the case), teaches precisely this tolerance and respect for the conscience of others.[4] Is this not the definition of secularism in education? Catholic teachers in the public schools fortunately realized this in time, and thanks to them, Christianity is represented in the schools in some proportion to the number of Christians in France as a whole. After some hesitations, their vocation is today recognized and highly esteemed by the hierachy.[5] It

[4] See the excellent book by Henri Chartreix, Au-delà du laïcisme (Editions du Seuil).

[5] "The thinking of Christian members of the teaching profession," declared Cardinal Feltin on March 28, 1961, "has contributed to the Catholic intellectual renewal; it has highlighted the richness and vitality of a doctrine which was condemned by many only in the caricature of it that was presented to them. The myth of the Church's obscurantism was doomed, and a strong blow struck at the triumph of scientism. . . . This was possible only because Christian teachers in the public schools discovered a true vocation in their teaching."

is not a second choice, as though the secular school were itself a necessary evil, but a proof that believers are capable, just like other people, of teaching in a way which does not offend any of the pupils, whether their families are religious, atheistic, or agnostic.

The action of these Catholic teachers in no way impairs the usefulness of the confessional teaching by which the Roman Church sets so much store.[6] Parents who wish to do so should be able to send their children to religious schools without excessive cost.[7] But from the point of view both of national unity and of the higher interests of the Church, it is desirable that Christians, both teachers and students, be present, on the same basis as others, in the public schools. Our French bishops have finally accepted

[6] Pluralism in education is necessary, on grounds of freedom of conscience, in a country which is religiously divided.

[7] On the express condition that these institutions justify their existence by the quality of the religious teaching which is offered there. This is far from being the general rule. We cannot think without anger of the Catholic schools where the religious instruction is lamentably poor. For proof, one has only to look at the results. In certain institutions for girls, in particular, there is sometimes a tendency to confuse religious instruction with the inculcation of certain moral taboos and the unhealthy cultivation of sentimental reflexes, to the exclusion of all intellectual training. Once out of school, life quickly shatters this tawdry instruction. Rarely, unless some exceptional grace intervenes, does anything fill the void thus created. And then people dare express surprise because the young are attracted to atheist existentialism!

Nevertheless, we must acknowledge that in the past few years the number of these establishments so little worthy to be called Christian has been decreasing, and that a real effort is being made to bring methods of religious instruction up to date.

this, and they now refrain from censuring Catholic parents who choose to send their children to secular schools.

It is up to Catholic parents to show themselves intransigent in the matter of religious education, and to demand qualified chaplains for these institutions. Petty quarrels have too often obscured the fact that the essence of the Church's mission is to teach religion, not mathematics or botany.

Provided due caution is exercised, and sectarian resistance on either side can be broken down, the new relationship between public and Catholic schools provided for by law should gradually bring about peace in the school question and the desired harmony between these two types of education, for the greater good of the nation and of the Church. More qualified chaplains on the one hand, more openness of mind and religious discretion on the other, will finally lead to peaceful coexistence between the Catholic and the public schools, after years of hole-and-corner struggle.

The Christian community of tomorrow cannot be like that of previous years. Christian institutions must allow secular institutions to develop without ill grace. What should it matter to them if their number decreases, provided the Gospel message is transmitted? Catholics are only too inclined to enter history backwards, and to cling to obsolete positions. It is to be hoped that they will understand, in the light of the lessons of the past, that it is better to turn change to account than to resist it. And it is also to be hoped that they will discover that they have no monopoly on truth. Their own divisions should incite them to greater humility.

The secular school and the secular state are incontestable signs of an irreversible advance. The school for all, like the state for all, is a victory for freedom of conscience.[8] A modern state whose members belong to diverse spiritual families should not favor any one of them, but should accept them all. Political authority and religious authority are autonomous and sovereign in their own spheres.[9]

It is this distinction, taught by the Church, which is really the foundation of true secularism. Why insist that the word "God" appear in a constitution or that it be inscribed on the lintel of a school where unbelievers are also supposed to feel at home? There is, of course, no valid morality in conflict with God, or even without God. But although the unbeliever

[8] "The secularism of the temporal is the juridical condition of the freedom of the act of faith," states M. Vialatoux.

[9] Cardinal Gerlier has stated that if secularism means "proclaiming the sovereign authority of the state in its temporal sphere . . . then this doctrine is fully in accord with the doctrine of the Church. If it were to mean the state's decision not to submit to any superior morality, then we should have to assert that such a thesis is dangerous, retrogressive, and false. Dangerous because it justifies the excesses of despotism and leads straight to dictatorship. Retrogressive because it takes us back to the conception of the pagan state from which Christianity had freed us." (In November 1945, the French episcopate had made a similar statement.)

may be unaware of it, the God of Christians can inhabit his heart provided he is open to the values of loyalty, liberty, and love. Why force a man of good faith who does not have the faith to live in a society bearing a Christian label?

The Christendom of the future will be a society of Christian inspiration superior, perhaps, to that of former times, in which the external signs of faith proliferated, but without necessarily having any connection with daily life. We read in the Gospels about the leaven in the dough. Is it not in the nature of leaven to be invisible and omnipresent?

Conclusion

Catholicism, the Religion of Tomorrow?

> Tradition is yesterday's progress;
> progress is tomorrow's tradition.
>
> Jean Guitton

AT EVERY religious crisis since the Renaissance, prophets of doom have announced the imminent death of Catholicism. In the nineteenth century, to go no further back, men of science and philosophers, carried away by technological discoveries and modernist theories, gravely explained that the Roman Church, its vision of the world and its dogmas, were irremediably lost. Intellect plotted against faith with all its inventive resources; uncommon strength of character was needed to resist this trend and to perceive some glimmer of hope behind Rome's fulminations. We have only to recall the final paragraph of Pius IX's *Syllabus,* anathematizing all who thought that "the Pope can and must compromise with progress and modern civilization."

Communism believed—and believes—it had dealt a death blow to all religions. According to Marx, religion "alienates" man; scientific materialism proves that God does not exist and that dogma is incompatible with reason. There has thus arisen the most gigantic atheist enterprise of all times; its scope must not be underestimated. Its influence extends throughout the world, and it has more than one-fifth of humanity under its heel. The attraction of Communism for the masses and elites alike is one of the major facts of our time. At best, this neopagan mystique helps to build up a religious indifference which is even more dangerous, perhaps, than persecution. It is therefore legitimate to ask whether the hour of decline has not struck for Christianity, and whether, in the more or less distant future, the religious phenomenon will not have become extinct.

However, it is necessary to examine honestly whether Christianity is really incapable of surviving this tidal wave; whether there is not, between Christianity and other religions, a difference in kind as well as in degree. Is it enough to place Christianity at the top of the list, or should it be in a category by itself?

For the believer, the answer is not in doubt. He knows that the gates of hell will never prevail against the Church, which has received from its founder the

Conclusion

promise of eternal life. But this faith for internal use could not convince the unbeliever, and it is from his point of view that we should like to evaluate Christianity's chances of survival.[1]

Let us first note a definite awakening of religious thought. Among Christian philosophers and theologians are men of great eminence, whom modern thinkers cannot ignore. In France and Germany, notably, this renewal is exceptional. At the same time, on the pastoral level, an impressive impetus has been given to different manifestations of religious life. In all areas of research (history, philosophy, theology, biblical exegesis, sociology) and of action (liturgy, methods of apostolate, politics), Christians are giving a good account of themselves. The divorce of intelligence and faith, which not so long ago was thought to be irremediable, is beginning to be regarded as something far less obvious. Atheism itself, as we have seen, is studied with understanding and sympathy by the most ardent believers, who realize what benefits religion can reap from it.

An attentive appraisal of the fundamental choices before the Church would seem to justify a certain optimism. For the Church contains within itself the antidotes to the errors which are harming it so

[1] "The true way to be a Christian at the present time," said Cardinal Gerlier, "is to put yourself in the unbeliever's place, to look with intelligent and fraternal sympathy at his difficulties, his objections, his indifference, and even his hostility."

greatly. The Church has always championed the inalienable rights of reason and its autonomy in relation to the sphere of faith. The Church teaches, for instance, that the existence of God is not a matter of faith, and that reason alone is capable of demonstrating it by its own powers. What greater tribute to reason could it pay? The Vatican Council, as we have seen, condemned "fideism," according to which man could not attain to any truth without the assistance of Revelation. The consequences of this position are incalculable.

In cases of disputes—and there has been no lack of them in the course of history—the last word rests indisputably with reason. Thus it was that the Church was forced to abandon naïve beliefs which had turned out to be untenable—for example, the cosmogony of the Bible, the direct creation of man's body by God, the supernatural explanation of certain psychosomatic anomalies such as alleged miracles or stigmata. There is every indication that more and more beliefs extraneous to the faith will be swept away with the advance of scientific biblical exegesis and depth psychology.

Monsieur Pouget proved himself to be a precursor by distinguishing clearly between the spirit of Christianity and the particular mentality which clothes it but which is not essential to it. By accepting this divestment; by initiating it, in fact (we have only to recall the Church's position with regard to the

Conclusion

Lourdes medical bureau), the Church opens its doors to healthy criticism. Its temporary objections are usually attributable to pastoral caution. What a contrast to the stubborn ostracism practiced by some sects! One can imagine what Lourdes, for instance, would have become in their hands!

The Church holds that faith and intelligence, both gifts of God, cannot contradict one another. It is hard to see how a religion so ready to submit to the exigencies of reason could disappear.

The great Christian mysteries are outside the scope of reason, since they express suprarational truths, that is, truths above reason, but certainly not contrary to reason. However imperfect and fluid the notion of the "supernatural" may be, it is made clear than an unbridgeable gulf separates the things of God from the things of man. The boundaries fixed for these two spheres may vary, but the diptych will always remain; were it otherwise, religion would have no more reason to exist. It would become a vague system of ethics, a philanthropism stripped of theological foundation. Such suicide, were it possible, would not benefit humanity, with its congenital thirst for the absolute.

Catholicism also possesses an antidote to its excessive legalism, which increasingly discourages modern minds with their love of freedom and spirituality. When tensions mount between "doctors" and "prophets," the prophets sooner or later come out on top. When one of the faithful realizes the need for some reform, when he wants to probe more deeply some point of dogma which has hitherto escaped notice, or to found a religious order, or to initiate a liturgical renewal, he always gets his way—provided he is right. For the Church, progress and "reaching for the impossible" are the very law of its being. What should an institution fear from the future when it professes that the spirit must triumph over the letter, that the mystic is more useful than the theologian, that the saint may do whatever he pleases at the prompting of grace? The Church is not an end in itself; it knows that it must serve the leaven of the Gospel. Its attachment to tradition is the expression of its perpetual capacity to renew itself and to become more faithful to its founder. Appearances notwithstanding, the Church is not against life, for, by its own definition, it is the living spouse of Christ, and desires to be attentive to the promptings of the Spirit.

But the Church takes the Incarnation seriously. It therefore believes in the need for a visible society, duly structured to bear, through the ages, the truths with which it has been entrusted, like a jar containing precious perfume. Hence its external apparatus, its rules, the intransigence of an organization both monarchical and collegial, without which—as experience has shown in the Reformed churches—unity is broken, disorder ensues, and the most sacred truths are distorted.

Conclusion

On the merely human level, the Roman Church gives proof of incomparable balance, coherence, and stability. Its qualities have enabled it to withstand the erosion of time. Thanks to a combination of realism and idealism, and to a dialectic of obedience and freedom, it has overcome all obstacles. Again and again it should have succumbed under the blows of its adversaries by reason of its failings, and again and again it has emerged victorious, with amazing recuperative ability. If the faithful quite rightly attribute this to the assistance of the Spirit, the outside observer regards it as a result of the Church's adaptability and its institutional genius. Secular governments could learn much from a study of ecclesiastical institutions, with their exceptional combination of severity and flexibility.[2]

The expression "the youthfulness of the Church" is in fashion. It points to the vitality of an institution which has defied time and remains full of promise. But might it not have another meaning too? Despite two thousand years of experience, is not the Roman Church in some ways still an adolescent who has not yet reached the maturity of the adult? Has it even reached adolescence?

Indeed, the Church may be only at the dawn of its existence, in the morning of its course among men. Like a babe whose umbilical cord is still imperfectly severed, it is linked to the environment which saw its birth—the Mediterranean shore. Since

[2] The importance of customary law in the Church is significant.

its birth, it has expressed itself in the concepts of Western civilization, although it is destined for all civilizations and belongs to none exclusively.[3] It acts, sometimes, like an emotionally disturbed child who fears independence, and clings desperately to positions seven hundred years old.

"You have stopped the clock of history in the sixteenth century, and you go on for ever and ever serving up the same soup," exclaims Giovanni Papini, addressing the theologians. "You have not got out of your petrified rut, your repetitions, your mechanical syllogisms, your cerebral and formalist pedantry. Your offices are full of scribes!"[4]

Like a child, the Church fears the wind of the open sea. It shields itself behind a shell of interdicts, and constantly falls back on authority, on rules. The traditionalist temptation is to create a bulwark against anxiety.[5] The Church likes to surround itself with people who are passively submissive and who are not likely to leave it alone in the dark. It fears unknown lands and new faces. It is suspicious of

[3] "The Church," wrote Pius XII on September 18, 1955, "is not identified with the Western cultures; it is not, in fact, identified with any one culture, but it is prepared to ally itself with all."

[4] Giovanni Papini, *Letters of Pope Celestine VI To All Mankind* (New York: E. P. Dutton and Co., 1948).

[5] Jean Piaget points out that, up to the age of seven, the child lives by an authoritarian moral code imposed from without, combined with an egocentrism which does not facilitate contact with others. "The authoritarian conscience," writes Friedrich Heer, "fears God and fears men, which is why it seeks to effect conversions and engages in proselytism, if necessary by force. It does not feel secure itself, and expresses its anxiety in this way."

Conclusion

turbulent laymen who would shake it out of its cherished habits—which are often no more than a preference for the easiest way. It wraps itself up snugly; it likes blinkers, which protect it from indiscreet glances. It dreads scandals, but does not reject *combinazioni* when they enable it to cover up certain deceptions.

Like children, the Church loves pomp, uniforms, fanfare, ceremonies, baroque bad taste, sentimental religious art. It returns blow for blow; it lets itself be drawn into sterile polemics; it rarely has the courage to turn the other cheek.

Another sign of youthfulness is that the Church is much more interested in the morality of the Ten Commandments than in that of the Beatitudes, which requires greater spiritual maturity. It is still frightened of the explosive force of the Gospel. It compromises with the powers that be. It has more faith in the virtues of diplomacy than in those of detachment. And there is such frequent talk in the Church about the need for an "adult faith" that one suspects that that faith must be somewhat puerile. The example sometimes comes from quite high up. In connection with the attacks made by Mgr. Romeo,[6] professor at the Lateran, on the alleged "progressive-

[6] The violence of these attacks aroused Rome, and Pope John was affected by it. He therefore asked the parties concerned to cease all public polemics; and to show his sympathy for the tendency under fire, he named Fr. Vogt, rector of the Pontifical Institute for Biblical Studies, to the post of consultant to the preparatory Theological Commission of the Council.

ness" of Catholic exegesis, Fr. Le Blond wrote in *Etudes*:

"We must deplore the fact that concern for security is openly substituted for respect for truth. This is the usual mask of traditionalism; an undeniably sincere attachment to the Church is compromised by fear, as though the Church needed to fear scientific research and the impartial striving after truth."

Even the jargon affected in the official Catholic Action movements—not in all youth movements—displays a grade-school mentality to be found among those who, as the saying goes, are just beginning to "set their wits to work."

A youthful Church? Yes, the Church is youthful in the best and in the worst acceptations of the term.[7] But it is beginning to be aware of it and to open its windows upon the world. It is beginning to appreciate the religious or secular values of "the others," and to abandon a dangerous narcissism.

It is no answer to atheistic Communism to call it "intrinsically perverse." It is no answer to the "godless" to call them satanical. It is no answer to an audacious book to put it on the Index. It is no an-

[7] A disconcerting paradox: this Church is in the hands of old men. Is it not tempting the Holy Spirit to entrust dioceses to octogenarians with life tenure? What human society could function under such conditions? In our times, when even men in the prime of life are overwhelmed by the rapidity of all kinds of change, it seems urgent to impose an inexorable age limit on all ranks of the hierarchy.

Conclusion

swer to the African or Asian civilizations to present them with a "white" Catholicism, cast in the mold of a civilization which they revile because it came to them in the baggage of the invader. The strong respect contradiction; they can appreciate differences and turn them to account—a difficult procedure, to be sure, but surely the only effective one, and also the only one which conforms to the Gospel.

The great merit of John XXIII was that he called upon the whole Church to reform itself, and to set about it with the severity required for an examination of conscience. Pope John finally reversed the current: instead of congratulating himself upon representing the only true Church, he asked Catholics to sweep their own doorstep and to turn their critical faculties in the first place upon themselves.[8]

Perhaps for the first time in history, a Pope called a Council which was not directed against anyone, unless the Church's own demons. These are named, as we have seen, pride, sloth, routine, vanity, author-

[8] It is significant that the instructions given by Pope Hadrian VI in 1522 to the apostolic nuncio in Germany were widely quoted in circles close to the Vatican during the pontificate of Pope John. The relevant passage reads: "You must say [before the Diet of Nuremburg] that we freely acknowledge that God has permitted the persecution of the Church because of the sins of men, and particularly of priests and prelates. . . . Therefore you will promise in Our Name that we shall devote all our energy to reforming, first of all, the court of Rome, whence perhaps all the evil sprang; the remedy will come from Rome, as it was from Rome that came the disease."

itarianism, contempt for non-Catholics, and the love of money, honors and temporal power,[9] and so on.

In this way, perhaps, and in any case only in this way, will the "separated brethren"—as they are still sometimes called, rather condescendingly—who rejected Catholicism for serious religious reasons, rediscover the possibility of an honest dialogue.

"If you want others to change, begin by changing yourself." How could so obvious a dictum have been so badly neglected? In this respect, the World Council of Churches—formerly cold-shouldered by Rome —sets a fine example. Its members are encouraged by one another to reform themselves, out of obedience to Jesus Christ. It is with relief that the Catholic finally sees his Church join humbly in the great ecumenical chorus.

"The Protestants," quipped Montesquieu, "will disappear, but by the time they do, Catholicism will have become Protestant!" The comment throws light on present developments within the two confessions. While the Reformed churches are rediscovering certain values which they had neglected out of reaction against Catholicism (tradition, liturgy, centralization, community life, participation in political life, etc.), the Roman Church is once more emphasizing points which had been virtually ignored since the Counter Reformation (study and dissemination of the

---

[9] "A little less politics," wrote Mgr. Roncalli in 1947 to the Bishop of Bergamo, "and a little more Christian fervor, would suffice to give life and efficacy to the apostolate."

Conclusion

Bible, freedom of conscience, personal religious life, subjective aspects of morality, attenuation of Marian devotion, sobriety of places of worship, etc.).

In any case—it is not superfluous to make the point —Catholicism would be enriched if ever Protestantism were willing to cohabit with it once more (it did, after all, for fifteen centuries), for its absence is cruelly felt. The Orthodox contribution would be equally precious to the Roman Church. Its emphasis on the spiritual and mystical would counterbalance any excessive emphasis on law and morals in the Roman Church. The price of every separation is the impoverishment of both parties.

But the reunion of the Christian Churches is not imminent. To imagine the contrary would reveal total ignorance of ecumenical difficulties or quite startling naïveté. John XXIII realized it better than anyone, and it is hard to see how the Council should provide the occasion for spectacular returns. In any case, the very word "return" understandably exacerbates Protestant, Anglican, and Orthodox susceptibilities. The schisms have lasted too long for any mere turning back to be possible. Divergent traditions have grown up which cannot be conjured away. Ecumenism has to be looked for in the future. It will be the fruit of long labor, and will require considerable intellectual and spiritual asceticism. The path of unity is strewn with pitfalls.

The important thing at this point is that the psychological climate should continue to improve and that the members of the different churches should approach each other with understanding and love. Considerable progress has already been made in this direction. The personality of Pope John made possible contacts which a few years earlier would have been considered impossible—for instance, with the Anglican Primate, or, on a lesser scale, with the Protestant community of Taizé.

As for the distant future, can unity be achieved in any other way than around a center? And that center, probably, in spite of everything, will be the Roman Church, genealogically linked with the primitive Church, and with a capacity for hospitality that is really unlimited, whatever people may say.

History shows that Catholicism has the stomach of an ostrich. The Roman doctrine contains so many contradictory elements, theologians possess such virtuosity, and, let us repeat, the Church has such genius for assimilation that we can already foresee possibilities of accommodation. And surely one of the purposes of the Council is precisely to prepare the way for unity by measures designed to remove some of the grounds for hesitation of the separated Churches. It is a striking fact that the reforms advocated by the Council Fathers often take the very direction desired by the non-Roman Churches.

Catholicism, the religion of tomorrow? Yes, to the extent that the Church takes to heart the tasks which

Conclusion

press upon it. Apart from spectacular moves in the area of poverty—when shall we see an end to Roman pomp and Vatican luxury, which constitute a real insult to the poor who make up two-thirds of humanity?[10]—an urgent intellectual reform, consisting in part of the reorganization and internationalization of the Curia, the reappraisal of the powers of the bishops, the extension of the rights of the laity, and a greater openness to non-Western civilizations, awaits the Church.

We have already quoted Fr. Dubarle, who asks for a vigorous purification of the faith in the name of science. Here is another, even clearer, statement by Canon Morel, former superior of the seminary of the Mission de France:

The faith today must take especial account of the universality of the technological field, in which there seems to be no limit to men's powers. . . . The Church cannot run away from this ever-growing sphere. It will approach it in the strength of the Holy Spirit . . . provided we do not shut ourselves up in our somnolent fears or our obsolete categories. A radical reorientation is required in this area, and required at once. The scientific approach, is already, and will increasingly become,

[10] Pope John did not like the *Sedia Gestatoria*, and used it as little as possible, preferring to move among the crowd on the same level as everyone else. "I do not want to look like an oriental satrap," he said.

199

the universal approach which will absorb all eth-
nic, local, cultural, racial, and other characteristics.
And why should not this approach be for our mid-
twentieth century what Roman civilization was in
the first centuries of our era—the providentially
prepared carrier of the Gospel? God did not choose
to appeal to men in the first place through their
feelings. Nor did he want to take them by force.
He appealed to their intelligence. God took a
chance—at first sight an apparently hopeless
chance, and certainly not a profitable one—on
making himself understood by men, by the men of
our day in particular, so avid for accuracy and
truth, so wary of being taken in by myths, however
consoling and reassuring they might be.

This necessary harmonizing of the official expressions of faith and modern science could have incalculable consequences. But the experts capable of
undertaking it are unfortunately few. Nevertheless,
the Church did have the good fortune to possess a
man like Fr. Teilhard de Chardin. The inevitable
imperfections of his achievement annoyed the theologians, who prefer to tilt at windmills, as Cardinal
Cushing put it, rather than to buckle down to the
real problems. But Catholic opinion as a whole has
endorsed the underlying movement of his thought.
Teilhard de Chardin's fundamental intuitions—he
would say it himself, with tranquil audacity—have

Conclusion

the future on their side, for they lie at the heart of our present difficulties. How many have left the Church because they were unable to square their religious faith with a scientific view of the world! And how many have returned to the Church upon coming into contact with the Jesuit scientist!

Spiritual schizophrenia is a hallmark of our age. Modern man has an emotional urge to believe—he knows intuitively that Christianity is irreplaceable—but he cannot reconcile his faith with the twentieth-century *Weltanschauung*.

With Teilhard de Chardin—who said of himself that he was as much a "child of the earth" as a "child of heaven"—came a possible remedy. He believed not only in the compatibility of Christianity and evolution, but also in the convergence and internal complicity of those two visions of the world. The supernatural, in his view, is no longer to be regarded as something artificially affixed upon nature, but as the reason for the existence of nature and the logical—and transcendent—goal of its strivings. Maurice Blondel had already sensed that grace, without ceasing to be a free gift of God, fitted into nature, where its place had been hollowed out, so to speak. Teilhard de Chardin transposed this intuition to the sphere of creation, in all its historical "thickness." In his view, material evolution serves the spirit, and the spirit serves unity and love. The modern scientific vision of the world gives Christianity a cosmic dimension, and Christianity, in its turn, gives a supreme meaning to all that has existed, that does exist, and that will exist.

Socialization held no terrors for Teilhard de Chardin. On the contrary, he welcomed it as a decisive step toward material and spiritual unity. He believed that a new civilization was in the making in which every indvidual would find untapped sources permitting a fuller development of his personality.

From the beginning, he maintained, the world has aspired toward unity. The historical Christ is at the center of evolution.[11] Toward him all things have converged, and the preparation of the "new heavens and the new earth" begins with him. At the end of time, the Son of God will come back to harvest creation like a fruit, a creation ripe for its ultimate metamorphosis.

The novelty of this scientifico-religious cosmology, which yet in certain respects is so traditional, caused the traditionalists to accuse Teilhard of confusing two distinct spheres of knowledge, and of preaching naturalism. The Christian people, however, instinctively saw in it an answer to their inarticulate longings. The popularity of his works is proof of it.

In other times, Teilhard de Chardin's work could have been officially utilized by the Church, which

11 The Roman liturgy goes so far as to say, with Isaia (45:8): "Let the earth be opened and bud forth a saviour" (Fourth Sunday of Advent).

would have derived great benefit from it. With his extraordinary love for matter, he did not reject materialism, but brought it into his system, connecting it with the spiritual life—and what more useful task could there be in our age? He offered a glorious philosophy to all who desire to work for the reorganization of the world and for human happiness.

It will probably be a long time before Teilhard de Chardin achieves full recognition in the Church. But the day is bound to come. The static and individualistic conceptions of religion which have been current since the Renaissance will finally be discarded like an outworn garment. And they will have to be replaced. Here the elaboration of a synthesis such as the one proposed by the author of *The Divine Milieu* becomes essential. It will be the work of some new St. Thomas Aquinas. Just as in the Middle Ages the Angelic Doctor brought Christianity into harmony with the pagan philosophy of Aristotle, so the theologian who is so anxiously awaited will have to bring Catholicism into harmony with science.

The survival of Western humanism is at stake, and, humanly speaking, of Christianity.

Catholicism, the religion of tomorrow? Why not?[12] What can surpass a religion centered upon love and

[12] Cournot maintains that there will be no more new religions, as there will be no new languages; the time of great creations of that kind is over, in his view. On this subject, see Jean Guitton, *L'Eglise et l'Evangile* (Editions Grasset), which contains many interesting observations on the future of Catholicism.

the deification of man? While the teaching of the *Imitation of Christ*, with its contempt for the world and sinful human nature, is already three-quarters dead, that of the Gospel and the Beatitudes seems immortal. Only Christianity can deliver man from his spiritual neuroses, for it gives meaning to his suffering, and teaches him to accept himself as a sinner. The Christian knows that he is known, personally loved, and redeemed by Christ. What an incomparable source of stability and joy! Moreover, his faith inspires him to collaborate, by his own effort, in the continuous creation of the world.[13]

The human animal, it seems, cannot do without religion. That is why Communism, which claims to be a mystique of humanity, is so successful. The time is no doubt near when Marxist ideology and Christianity will find themselves face to face, alone, as the only two valid "religions" on this planet.[14] Then the "new Middle Ages" heralded by Nicholas Berdyaev will have arrived. The Russian philosopher believed that the Renaissance era was about to perish, and that a new religious era of humanity was dawning. Will Communism in its atheistic form survive for

13 See Fr. M. D. Chenu, *La theologie du travail* (Editions du Cerf).

14 Jean Guitton writes: "The option confronting us, as Newman foresaw, is between radical atheism and the least adapted, least accommodating religion; between a philosophy which negates the most and one which affirms, and therefore demands, the most. . . . It is possible that the atheist world surrounding us is more vulnerable than any other."

Conclusion

long? Nothing is less certain. The future may see it come to grief like every other doctrine of violence,[15] whereas it is hard to see what could kill a doctrine which issues in nonviolence. In this respect, too, Catholicism is still in its infancy. When will Christians finally assimilate the lesson of Gandhi? The atomic bomb could do the West the terrible service of demonstrating the absurdity of armed violence. In all probability, Rome will one day—better late than never—lead a crusade of collective conscientious objection.

[15] Pope John XXIII spoke of Communism in these prophetic terms, admirable in their humility, restraint, and serenity:

"Yes, we are facing the giant Goliath, and perhaps we waste too much time talking which could be better used praying or laying down rules for our own sanctification and that of our neighbors. We are facing someone who seems to us enormous; but he is not strong, he is not healthy, for he is the expression of error, greed, violence. Sometimes we feel fear invade us and the thought of the morrow fills us with dread. And yet this giant will have to yield before the will, the grace, the mercy of God. And we should not think that the victory of this Goliath would necessarily bring with it universal destruction and ruin, because even in such times of subjugation there are souls nourished by the same light as we are, who remain faithful and very close to us, sharing in the same Christian and apostolic ideal.

"The simplicity of the young David standing up to the giant truly represents the Catholic Church, holy and blessed. It represents the glorious handful of our athletes advancing humbly, united in their holy endeavors, comforted and exultant in the thought that they are followed by magnificent hosts. . . .

"Let the giant advance with his immense threat. Like the youth of Bethlehem, the sons of the Church of Christ, religious and lay alike, will meet him in the strength of God."

Catholicism, the religion of tomorrow? Yes, if we remember that man is in process of rediscovering, by the resources of his intellect, the cogency of the great religious truths[16]—the truth that man has an almost biological need for spirituality, that the need to adore is inscribed in the depths of his nature; the truth that prayer is the health of the soul; the truth that sacrificial love of neighbor, and detachment, have a wonderfully stabilizing effect; the truth that the great religious myths issuing from the collective unconscious have a profound significance. The advance of depth psychology works in the long run in favor of Christianity, and can be turned to account to strengthen its positions.[17] Man's happiness, science tells us today, does not reside in material comfort alone. The work of Dr. Chauchard, the neurophysi-

[16] "The existence of science gives Christians a bad conscience," wrote Simone Weil. "Very few of them dare be sure that if they started from scratch, and if they considered every problem, suppressing all preference, in an absolutely impartial spirit of exploration, Christian dogma would appear to them as manifestly and totally true."

[17] See in particular the works of C. G. Jung. They show that the religious instinct is basic to man, and they help explain the meaning and scope of the great religious mysteries. Shortly before his death, the great psychoanalyst confided to a journalist: "What is sometimes called instinct or intuition is none other than God. God is the voice of our conscience. . . . In our somber atomic century, where fear stalks everywhere, man seeks a guide. Consciously or unconsciously, he has set out once more on his blind quest for God. All that I have learned has brought me step by step to an unshakable conviction: God exists. I do not have faith in God; I know that he exists."

Conclusion

ologist, a disciple of Teilhard de Chardin, demonstrates that the brain is fully utilized only if man adapts himself to the great principles of Christian morality. Jean Rostand declares: "Science teaches us to love all men. This is where it joins Christianity. Psychology states, for example, that maternal love is necessary for the education of children, and shows that eight out of ten neuroses are due to a lack of love. The sick person is one who cannot overcome his egocentrism, arrive at altruism, at self-sacrifice. Love is the higher stage of the evolution of the instincts. A man who loves will never go mad. Science has rehabilitated love."[18]

The convergence of the conclusions of science and certain of the teachings of religion is beginning to be quite striking. A twofold movement is taking place before our sometimes inattentive eyes. While the Church is disposed to become more open to the world, to understand its needs, the world is imperceptibly drawing closer to the Church. Thus the distance between them is diminishing, notwithstanding appearances and the survival of prejudices. It is reasonable to suppose that this rapprochement will continue in the years to come. Atheism itself, as we have seen, can serve the cause of religion by its

[18] See also Marc Oraison, *Devant l'angoisse et l'illusion* (Editions Fayard), in which the author seeks to show that there is a certain harmony between the truths of faith and some fundamental aspects of human psychology brought to light by Freud.

exigencies. People like Camus, or even Sagan—impenitent moralists that they are—are surely, in their own way, and along with many others, a species of catechumen without faith.[19]

The extraordinary "International" of Catholicism is both the first nucleus of world unification and the best artisan of its spiritual liberation. Technology too, a product of science—which is also essentially universal—is working at an ever more rapid cadence toward the material unification and liberation of the world. This twofold labor would seem to be complementary.

The secular values of the world, after violently opposing Catholicism, are drawing closer to it.[20] We have already spoken of the gradual broadening of the content of natural morality. These signs are of the greatest importance, for the Church and the world need each other for their true fulfillment. For if technology is the material salvation of the world (it feeds the hungry), and if the Church is the spiritual salvation of the world (it reveals to the world that it has been redeemed by the God-Man), the world is the health of the Church. Without it, the Church would

[19] We have to give credit to an era which has heard Camus exclaim: "For me, the only concrete problem I know of today is whether one can be a saint without God."

[20] Cardinal Montini put it in striking fashion: "The world, which advances, seeks, and suffers, is unwittingly walking backwards toward Christ." That is to say that every man of good will, though he be an atheist, draws closer to God even if he is unaware of it, even if he thinks he is moving away from God.

Conclusion

have no reason to exist, it would not understand itself, it would shrivel up, like shagreen.[21]

In 1957, Cardinal Montini declared to the Congress of the Lay Apostolate: "The Church's mission is to establish contact between the sacred and the profane in such a way that the former is not contaminated but communicated, and the latter is not distorted but sanctified."

The dialectics of the relations between the world and the Church could not be better defined. Emergent Christianity, as we pointed out in our discussion of secularism, succeeded in "desacralizing" the world. This process must be followed by a "consecration of the world." The expression was dear to Pius XII, who used it on the occasion of the same Congress of the Lay Apostolate. For it is the duty of the laity to permeate the world with Christian values, with the discretion required of apostles of spiritual freedom; not so much by forming new, specifically Christian institutions, as by their witness in all secular groups.

The dogma of the Incarnation, which sees in Christ, the new Adam, one who is both truly God and truly Man, expresses this mysterious relationship between sacred and profane. The Church offers

[21] Its dialogue with the world can only bring the Church enrichment and greater self-knowledge. Cardinal Léger wrote in June 1961: "The man who cannot engage in dialogue is in danger of falling prey to fanaticism. To destroy dialogue means not only to eliminate the other, but to destroy oneself."

human endeavor an ideal of incomparable grandeur —to build up the mystical body of Christ, to fill up what is lacking of the sufferings of Christ, who died to give life to the world. The success of this mission depends in the end on the good will of the individual, since God does not refuse his grace to anyone, whether or not he belongs to the visible Church.

Catholicism, the religion of tomorrow? Viewed in this light, the answer is not in doubt. The special instrument of the world's spiritual unity, a religion which posits the evangelical equation that love of God equals love of neighbor, cannot die before the extinction of the human race. Despite its betrayals, the Church follows imperturbably the path mapped out for it by its founder. Sure of his trust and sure of the glorious destiny of a world which it knows is grafted in God, it will always find artisans to accomplish its mission, even if their number is dwindling temporarily.[22]

What can destroy a religion capable of drawing its substance from all aspects of reality, not rejecting a single one? Sin itself has served as a springboard, ever since the cross was planted on Golgotha.

The building of the visible Church will continue to the end of time. Twenty centuries from now, its

[22] The over-all increase in the number of Christians is not at the present time proportionate to that of the world's population as a whole, even though the Catholic Church is gaining in the United States, Britain, the Scandinavian countries, and parts of Africa.

Conclusion

appearance will be altogether changed, just as the Church today looks altogether different from the Church of the first centuries of our era. That is the law of progress. But behind all these changes of form, language, tradition, the same creative sap of freedom and love flows on from century to century.

Like hope, that virtue planted ineradicably in the heart of man, the Church represents the will to live of all creation, a creation in quest of self-transcendence.[23]

[23] "For creation was made subject to vanity—not by its own will but by reason of him who made it subject—in hope, because creation itself also will be delivered from its slavery to corruption in the freedom of the glory of the sons of God" (Romans 8:21-22).

Epilogue

It is a fact of experience that where contradictions abound, there also flowers the fairest hope.

Ignatius of Loyola

AT THE conclusion of this rapid survey, the exceptional complexity of Catholicism stands out, perhaps, more clearly. Of all institutions, the Roman Church is the one most fraught with contradictions.[1] Not only because it is made up of cockles and wheat, of sinners and saints, embodying, like its founder, the Spirit in the flesh, but also because its universal vocation obliges it to be present everywhere, in space

[1] Suzanne de Dietrich, a Protestant, one of the founders of the Ecumenical Institute of Bossey, once said to me: "It is in the Catholic Church that one finds the best and the worst."

and time. Therefore it constantly opens its arms throughout the centuries to all races and nations, testing all things and retaining what is good. Just as sacred art reinvents its forms in every age, so Christian doctrine is confronted in every age with the ideas of the times, and rejuvenated by the contact.[2]

The Church has said everything—Revelation has been closed for nineteen centuries—and yet everything remains to be worked over and delved into to the end of time.

Like the world, the Church is in constant process of formation. The Holy Spirit renews the face of the earth, and everything—fortunately—is grist to his mill.

[2] Teilhard de Chardin observed that in the first century, Christianity had entered the arena of human thought "by boldly assimilating Jesus to the Alexandrian Logos." He suggested a similar process in the twentieth century, "no longer with the regulative principle of the stable Greek cosmos, but with the neo-Logos of modern philosophy, the evolutionary principle of a universe in motion."